The Mystic Path of Meditation

Beginning a Christ-Centred Journey

The Mystic Path of Meditation

Beginning a Christ-Centred Journey

David Cole

ANAMCHARA BOOKS

Anamchara Books
220 Front Street
Vestal, New York 13850 U.S.A.

9 8 7 6 5 4 3 2 1

ISBN: 978-1-937211-86-8
ebook ISBN: 978-1-937211-87-5

Author: David Cole

Book design and production by Vestal Creative Services,
www.vestalcreative.com.

Printed in the UK.

This book is dedicated
first and foremost to my wife Amber,
who has been a constant companion through so much,
and also to my children, Edana and Elijah,
who teach me about joy, patience, and inspiration.

All to the glory of Elohim.

Contents

Learn to be peaceful,
and thousands around you will find salvation....
There is nothing better than peace in Christ,
for it brings victory over all the evil spirits
on earth and in the air.
When peace dwells in a person's heart, it enables him
to contemplate the grace of the Holy Spirit from within.
Those who live in peace
collect spiritual gifts as it were with a scoop,
and shed the light of knowledge on others.
All our thoughts, all our desires, all our efforts,
and all our actions should make us say constantly ...
"O Lord, give us peace!"'
When people live in peace,
God reveals mysteries to them.

—*Seraphim (nineteenth-century monk)*

I've discovered something, something that many people don't ever find, which is hidden in plain sight. I've discovered a path, an ancient path, a path on which, if you walk it, you will find rest for your soul.

Let me show you. . .

Foreword

In *Seeds of Contemplation*, Thomas Merton wrote that "contemplation is the highest expression of man's intellectual and spiritual life. It is that life itself, fully awake, fully active, fully aware that it is alive. It is spiritual wonder. It is spontaneous awe at the sacredness of life."

And yet too few of us have nourished this aspect of our natures. Without it, we are incomplete. As Alan Torey said, "There is a contemplative in all of us, almost strangled but still alive, who craves enjoyment of the Now and longs to touch the seamless garment of silence which makes us whole."

The contemplative in us has become strangled by the incessant demands of our consumer society, and modern life has become much ado about nothing. The church has colluded with this mind-set, and its members have become drained by the sheer work of "keeping things going." Too often, the church has marginalised and feared meditation, or falsely taught that it is not biblical. David Cole is an evangelical mystic who is restoring meditation to its rightful place. This book is an excellent contribution to this end.

In the first part of this book, he explains why we need a mystic path, and he disarms conservative Christians by setting out a biblical basis for meditation. In the second part, he breaks down meditation into small, practical chunks with which even the busiest person can engage. Personally, I suggest that you display these words on your kitchen or bedroom wall:

- meditate momentarily
- divert daily
- withdraw weekly
- make a date monthly
- abdicate annually

David teaches us how to link prayer with our breathing, read the Bible in a meditative way (lectio divina), undertake self-examination, use creation as a tool, become mindful in each thing we do, and use one word or phrase as a prayer focus. He provides practical exercises for all types of person. He also suggests ways adults can interest children in meditation, and he delightfully describes how he teaches his own children to fruitfully meditate.

I live on Lindisfarne, where I find many contemplative role models from Celtic history. This working island became known as Holy Island because in the seventh century its busy, fractious community was led by Cuthbert, who snatched times of meditation on the little islet now named after him. A local monk wrote: "Cuthbert dwelt also according to Holy Scripture, following the contemplative amid the active life." Later, Cuthbert was freed to live alone on the Inner Farne Isle, which I see from my window. The historian Bede writes of this period in Cuthbert's life: "He finally entered into the remoter solitude he had so long sought, thirsted after, and prayed for. He was delighted that after a long and spotless active life he should be thought worthy to ascend to the stillness of Divine contemplation." Even during these years of sustained solitude and meditation, however, Cuthbert "stormed the gates of heaven," and then emerged to spend two tireless years as a prophetic, evangelising bishop.

Meditation results in impact.

This book is a wonderful start to the path of meditation. There is no telling where our journey will end.

Ray Simpson
Founding Guardian of the Community of Aidan and Hilda
www.aidanhilda.org

Introduction

The deep peace of the quiet earth to you;
The deep peace of the still air;
The deep peace of the running wave to you;
The deep peace of the warming sun;
The deep peace of the gentle night to you;
The deep peace of the shining stars;
The deep peace of forgiving heart to you;
The deep peace of the Prince of Peace.
—*Celtic blessing*

Peace is hard to find sometimes. Our world is full of stress and tension. Stress surrounds us everywhere we turn—and we absorb it and make it part of our own hearts, minds, and bodies. We carry it with us wherever we go.

The practice of meditation offers an alternative. Regular meditation allows us to maintain an ongoing sense of inner calm. No matter how stressful our workload, no matter how much the children are driving us crazy, no matter how frustrating our roommate or boss, our mother or spouse may be, no matter *what* happens, the practice of meditation allows us to remain at peace. We don't have to wait for the relief of the end of the workday or the start of the holiday; we can have peace all the time now. We can carry peace with us wherever we go.

The path of meditation is a long one; if you decide to travel far on it, there are other books out there that can help you go further and deeper. This book is intended for those who are just starting the journey or who have never been able to find the path at all. It is for those who have never even realised that the path was there for them to take.

Take your time as you read this book. It's not meant to be read from front to back in one go. Instead, wend your way through it. The path it leads you down is meant to be a slow amble on a beautiful day rather than a hurried dash to the destination. As you read this book, my prayer is that it will help you grow in your relationship with God as you reclaim a vital practice that's been missing from your spiritual walk.

The Hebrew word for peace is *shalom*, but the word conveys far more than simply peace. According to *Strong's Concordance*, shalom means completeness, wholeness, health, safety, prosperity, fullness, rest, and harmony, as well as tranquillity and peace. This is the sort of peace that meditation offers. Meditation enables us to be whole and healthy, the people we were created to be. It allows us to find harmony with our own hearts, with those around us, and with the Divine.

That is my wish for you: Shalom!

David Cole
Autumn 2012

Part 1

Why We Need
the Mystic Path

1

What Is Meditation?

If you have not yet begun to meditate,
I implore you by the love of our Lord,
not to deprive yourself of so great a good.
There is nothing to be afraid of;
there is everything to gain.
—*Teresa of Avila*

I am a frequent visitor to a very beautiful place, the Holy Island of Lindisfarne in the northeast of England. I work for a Christian Celtic community—the Community of Aidan and Hilda—whose administration office and retreat centre is on the Island, which gives me a good excuse to visit. Even before I joined the Community, though, I visited the Island each year for a retreat.

During the holidays, especially the hot ones, the Island is teaming with tourists. They visit the castle and priory ruins, as well as the lovely open land and beaches. When you're on retreat, seeking a time of silence and reflection, it can be hard to find a space to be quiet. Over the years, however, I have found various places that are sheltered not only from the elements (which can be helpful when you are on an island off the northeast coast of England) but also from the tourists' noise and bustle. Some of these quiet spots I have found on my own, but those who know the Island well guided me to other sheltered, peaceful places.

One of these spots is "the prayer seats"—a couple of alcoves in the side of a cliff. During World War II, these were apparently used to store hidden ammunition; now they are good places to hide if you are seeking solitude and quiet. Without guidance and careful instruction, however, I would never have found them.

Near what is known as Saint Cuthbert's Beach is a hill called the heugh. From here, the steep path leads up to an old Coast Guard lookout. On one side of the heugh, down a steep slope, are the remains of the Benedictine priory; on the other side is a cliff face that drops to a rocky beach. One day, a dear friend of mine led me along the uneven path up the heugh, and then about halfway up, he turned onto a smaller trail that was barely wider than my foot. I would never have seen it if he had not pointed it out to me. I followed him obediently, though it looked as though we were heading over the edge of the cliff!

As we went further along the narrow path, I noticed two things. First, the path began to flatten out and widen (a little)—and second, the sounds of the rest of the world faded away. Once we reached the prayer seats, the alcoves in the cliff edge protected us from the noise of life. We looked out across the sea to the mainland of England, and the only sounds were the lap of the water and the cries of gulls and fulmars. Seals swam below us, poking their dark heads above the surface of the North Sea, and eider ducks bobbed on the waves.

Each time I go to Lindisfarne now, I seek this place of solitude and quiet. I take the path that is almost hidden, which looks as though it might lead to danger and trouble, but I know, because someone I trusted led me there—someone who was familiar with the path—that in fact it leads to a place of solitude and stillness. There, my heart and soul and spirit can connect with God without the distractions of life. I can sit there for hours and not see another person. For me, this is an ideal place for meditation.

Meditation is one of those words that conjure up different images. Some of us may picture ourselves cross-legged, fingers in a circle, humming; others may see ourselves sitting in silence while we struggle to cease the constant noise of our own thoughts; while still others may envisage happy gurus floating in the air in the lotus position. And some of us may envision meditation as something dark, occult, and dangerous.

Once, when I ran an ad for a relaxation and meditation class I was offering, a fairly conservative Christian contacted me, very concerned that I would be leading people into "emptying themselves" in such a way that (to use her words) "the evil one can get in." If this were to happen, she warned, "he is very hard to get out again." Somehow, meditation has gotten a bad name with conservative Christians. They see it as a distinctly un-Christian activity, rather than as a practice that might support their faith. They connect it to mysticism.

And in fact, as the title of this book suggests, that is an accurate connection. Meditation is a mystical experience.

I have a cat—a black cat with deep green eyes that sometimes seem to pierce my very soul. When we got her, we discussed as a family a few different names, and eventually settled on a name I had suggested—"Mystic." The fact that I now have a black cat named Mystic who has soul-piercing green eyes has caused a few raised eyebrows among fundamental Christians. To be honest, although the whole family agreed the name suited our cat, I did kind of suggest it *because* I knew what kind of reaction the name would cause in certain circles. I'm afraid it's the rebel in me! I know that in the minds of many folks, mysticism is associated with the occult, with the world of magic and dark powers.

But in fact, the true meaning of the word "mystic" points to practices I wholeheartedly endorse. According to the dictionary, a mystic is "one who, through meditation and contemplation, seeks to become of one mind and will with Deity." Based on this definition, then, all who seek to truly follow Christ should strive to be mystics. If we are followers of Christ, should not our everyday desire be to become like God? To be of one mind and will with God?

There have always been mystics who followed the ways of Christ; Christianity's spiritual heritage is rich with mysticism. The twelfth through the fourteenth centuries are often thought of as the "golden age" of Christian mysticism, the era during which the likes of Meister Eckhart, Julian of Norwich, and Thomas Aquinas had their day, not to mention the anonymous writer of *The Cloud of Unknowing*. But mysticism is not a fluke peculiar to this period of history; earlier mystics such as John Cassian of the fourth century and John Scotus Eriugena from the ninth, as well as modern mystics like Carl McColman (author of *The Big Book of Christian Mysticism*), show us that mysticism is—and always has been—a part of Christianity.

Meditation is a discipline—a practical practice—that helps us become mystics. It gives us a means by which we can seek to become one in mind and will with the Divine. Meditation is, in fact, a path that leads us to union with God. Buddhism may be the faith tradition many of us connect most closely to meditation, but in reality, meditation is not linked to any particular belief. Instead, it is a practice that creates a space in our lives— a sanctuary—where we deeply connect with something deeper and larger than ourselves.

So what exactly *is* meditation?

It is simply the practice of quieting the mind—the inner self—using techniques in sitting, breathing, and concentrating. It describes a state of concentrated attention on some object, thought, or word (a "mantra"). Meditation usually, but not always, involves turning the attention inward, but attention outward to music or visual imagery is also a common and useful practice. By focusing our minds, we draw in a sense of God—or, to look at it from a slightly different perspective, we extend our inner senses out to connect with God's Spirit around us. Meditation can be used both for personal development and to focus the mind on God—and both uses can draw us closer to God and enable us to engage more deeply with the Divine image that dwells within us.

Meditation is not something that is just for those who are super holy—or for those who are super stressed-out either! It is something all of us need; it's as normal and necessary as sleep. Sleep, after all, is not only for those who are completely exhausted nor is it an esoteric practice engaged in by a select group of skilled initiates. Instead, all of us (usually) sleep during every twenty-four-hour period. If we don't, our mind and bodies suffer. Meditation does for the mind, spirit, and soul what sleep does for the body. It renews our mental and spiritual resources. It prevents us from "burning out."

Meditation is also a form of prayer, closely linked to contemplative prayer. While some prayer is primarily an activity of the intellect, one that involves active thinking as we tell God what we want, meditation is a practice that involves acquiring an inner stillness where we simply be with God. It allows us to find internal silence even when we are in the midst of external noise. It is a path to the quiet, secret presence of God.

At first, this path may seem faint and hard to find; some may tell us that it leads to danger and trouble. But people we can trust have gone this way before. They know this path leads to a place where hearts and minds can connect with God, a quiet place protected from life's distractions. Here, in this sheltered space, we can become one with God.

2

Longing for God

The soul must long for God
in order to be set aflame by God's love;
but if the soul cannot yet feel the longing,
then it must long for the longing.
To long for the longing is also from God.
—*Meister Eckhart*

The path of my spiritual journey has been circuitous. I didn't set out on it with any sense that I was following a straight road that led directly to Christ.

As a child, I was brought up in a fairly restrictive conservative "free" evangelical church (a bit of an oxymoron!). I learned the Bible's stories with the aid of "flannel graph" pictures, and I was taught that Jesus died on the cross so I could get to heaven when I died; that belief in this was what separated believers from unbelievers; and that unbelievers were going to hell, unless they came to believe in Jesus in the way my church said they should. Despite this instruction in conservative, evangelical theology, I had no firsthand experience of anything spiritual. By my mid-teens, I was feeling despondent about the church as an organisation, and the people who belonged to it. I spread my spiritual wings the best I could: by flying off in any direction that seemed the opposite from what my church claimed was the "right" way.

This led me into various spiritual activities. I became particularly interested in the Pagan Celtic pattern of spirituality; I joined a ghost-hunting group and had various Pagan and Wiccan friends. During these years, I had many spiritual experiences, not all of which were good, but one thing I did discover: the practice of centring myself, being at one with "the spirit" (the general energy of the Cosmos and Universe), being at peace within myself.

After a few years on this path, I had the most intense spiritual experience I had ever had. I have no words to describe this encounter; all I know is that I was convinced I had been with Jesus.

This caused me some problems. Because of my experiences growing up, I had consciously rejected Jesus and the Christian God as rubbish and false. My mind fought with my heart. Intellectually, I was sceptical, but my heart was convinced beyond doubt that it had been with Jesus. If we are open-minded, our hearts generally win out over our heads; in my case, I surrendered myself to follow Christ. I concluded that it was "church," rather than Christ, that had made me struggle. In time, I started to study Christian Celtic spirituality and Christian mysticism. I saw within these a path toward both peace and a total centring on Christ.

As I got more and more involved in full-time Christian work, however, I noticed that many of those around me were burned out, teetering on the edge of some kind of emotional breakdown. This seemed strange to me. *If Jesus promises us freedom,* I wondered, *and a "light burden"—if the Bible promises us the peace of God that is beyond our understanding—why are so many of these full-time workers for Christ experiencing such emotional turmoil?* I looked to see if there was any pattern in these folks' experience. There was.

All those who felt "burned out"—or on the edge of that state of collapse—were those who never took time out from their busy lives to simply *be* with God. Instead, they were always on the go, constantly trying to squeeze more into a twenty-four-hour day. Meanwhile, all those who were able to ride the flow of life took time to be alone and quiet with God.

As I became more and more convinced that finding spaces of silence and calm alone with God was the answer, the key to living a full and balanced life, I remembered those people from my past who had seemed so tranquil and full of peace. They had practised certain techniques that allowed them to achieve this calm state of mind. I began to study these techniques, while I considered whether they were compatible with Christianity.

I found that many places in the Bible tell us to "meditate" and retreat from the world. I became convinced that mediation was a gift from God, a normal, healthy part of our spiritual lives. It had been removed from many forms of Christianity to their detriment. As I read and studied more, I also began to practise meditation. Eventually, I taught classes and workshops on it. I wanted to share with others what I had learned.

I became convinced that Christ's followers are not living in the fullness of their relationship with the One True God (Father, Christ, and Holy Spirit) if they neglect the practice of meditation. This is a practice that the Bible commands us to follow, a habit actively practised by Jesus himself. In fact, if we do not practise Christ-centred meditation and contemplative prayer, we are turning our backs on something God gave us because we need it. We need to reclaim meditation as a Christian practice, one whose proper spiritual usage enables us to have a complete and full relationship with God.

Meditation is often something associated with religions or faiths other than Christianity. Although there are a growing number of books and resources that enable us to know that meditation is acceptable within the Christian faith, according to Brian Hedges of Life Action Ministries, one in every 10,000 Christians meditate regularly. If Hedges' claim is true, my guess is that the majority of the other 9,999 Christians may view meditation as something that's contrary to their faith. As a result of this misunderstanding, followers of Christ have been robbed of something special, sacred, and practical. Meditation enables us to develop a deeper more authentic relationship with

God. It creates a channel through which the Divine image within us can truly and deeply connect with the Great Divine.

Meditation is a truly biblical concept as well. The word "meditate" or a derivative appears at least sixty times in the Bible. "Do not let this Book of the Law depart from your mouth; meditate on it day and night," God told Joshua (1:8 NIV); the psalmist wrote, "My eyes stay open through the watches of the night, that I may meditate on your promises" (119:148 NIV); "Meditate upon these things," Paul advised Timothy, "give yourself wholly to them; that your progress may appear to all" (1 Timothy 4:15 KJ2000).

Christ himself withdrew regularly to a quiet place to spend time with God (Luke 5:16). According to Zondervan's *New International Exhaustive Concordance*, the Greek word for "withdrew" in this verse is *eimi-hypochoreo*, a word that means more than just hiding away from life's hustle and bustle. In Luke 5, we read that life was indeed pressing against Jesus, but he was not stepping behind a rock to catch his breath or even to have what we might call a "quiet time." The Greek word splits into two words: *eimi*, which means "to be," and *hypochoreo*, which means "to retreat"—so the word literally means to retreat from life to simply be. In other words, Jesus made a regular practice of stepping out of the busy world in which he was engaged and deliberately set aside time to be with the Father. We too, if we are to follow Jesus' example, need to engage ourselves in the regular practice of making space and time in our lives to be with God.

We retreat from the world in order to make room for God in our hearts. This is what happens during meditation, and it is different from "daily Bible reading" or any other practice that is primarily intellectual. Instead, meditation is a time of intimacy with the One who loves us best. Just as lovers yearn for each other's presence, we are created with a God-longing deep in our hearts. And in the same way that lovers need times when they close the door on the rest of the world, we too need spaces where we can focus wholly on our deepest and truest Love.

3

Letting Our Souls Catch Up

Like the Sabbath,
meditation is not about making
or changing anything,
or feeling a special way,
but just waking up, in a focused way,
to what's already here.
Just be.
Serve God not in changing the world,
but in relaxing into what's already there.
—Jay Michaelson

A few years ago, the American comedian Dave Allen remarked: "We spend our lives on the run: we get up by the clock; eat and sleep by the clock; and go to work on the clock, and then you retire, and what do they give you? A CLOCK!"

Time rules our lives. As a result, instead of travelling along enjoying life's ride, many of us travel with the express purpose of getting to our destination. We have to meet our next deadline, whatever that might be, while we do our best to squeeze as much as possible into our lives. Our lives these days are like cars speeding along a motorway, rather than taking a slow scenic ride for the pure pleasure of the ride. Direct access to the destination is our goal! Even when we do pause for a moment, we behave more as if we were pulling into a service station for some fast food than stopping to enjoy the scenery and a good meal. We feel a constant pressure to move faster, get more done, and do it more quickly. The more we can get done in a shorter space of time, the better we think we are, as though someone somewhere will be awarding prizes for speed and sheer number of achievements. We drive fast and we walk fast—even on our days off from work—because there's just *so much to be done.*

One of the things you can get away with as an adult when you have children is watching children's movies; often, I've noticed, some profound truths are embedded in these films. In the Disney/Pixar movie *Cars*, the main character Lightning McQueen (voiced by Owen Wilson) is a young, energetic race car totally focused on being the fastest and winning the "Piston Cup." His friend, Sally Carrera, a Porsche 911 (voiced by Bonnie Hunt), points out to him the difference between how things are now on the road compared to the days before super highways: "Cars didn't drive to *make* good time, they drove to *have* a good time." We too have lost this ability. Our lives are all about *making* good time rather than *having* a good time.

Our lives are imbalanced, and our hearts, minds, and bodies have fallen out of equilibrium. We do too much, and we rest too little. Sue Palmer, who studies the behaviour of children, suggests in *Toxic Childhood* that one of the reasons children are facing so many problems today (she quotes the American Psychological Association, which estimates that one in five children have mental health problems) is that "our culture has evolved faster than our biology." In other words, technology allows our lives to move faster than our bodies and minds can handle.

I heard a story once about some Westerners who arrived in the thick jungle of some undeveloped country and hired locals to carry their equipment. The Westerners then proceeded to travel at such a pace that eventually, the locals dropped the equipment and sat down, refusing to move. Finally, when the Westerners couldn't get the locals up and moving, they asked the interpreter to find out why the people had come to a halt. The locals replied, "We have moved so fast so far that we have to stop to allow our souls to catch up."

This is exactly what Palmer is talking about in her book—and if we look into our own minds and hearts, we will probably discover we are each experiencing the same sort of thing. Life has moved so fast that our souls have been left behind. We feel out of balance. Our emotional and physical health may be suffering as a result.

Meditation is a way to step out of the rat race, a technique for slowing down so that our souls can catch up. It allows us to find the inner balance we need to face life. It allows us to not only unwind but to truly relax.

There's a difference between unwinding and relaxing. In a wind-up watch, the spring is wound very tightly, much like we are in our everyday lives. As the watch ticks, the spring unwinds. We too may find space to unwind in our day, reading a book or watching the television. But an unwound spring within a watch is not relaxed. If we were to remove the spring from a watch and heat it, allowing the metal to go back to its natural state, it would become flat. In a similar way, meditation brings us into a deeply relaxed state, which is much deeper and more natural than just unwinding. Without these times, if we keep going without stopping, eventually we can no longer "unwind" the tension within us. Something within us—physically or emotionally—will break, at least temporarily.

Psalm 46:10 says, "Be still and know that I am God." The Hebrew word that's translated "still" also means "slack." In other words, be like a rope that's been pulled tight and now has been released so that it hangs loose. Let go of the tension that has wound you up.

An old story illustrates this same point:

> There was once a wise old monk who was meditating in the forest, enjoying the creatures and creation around him. A hunter who knew the monk came across him in the forest. "Why are you wasting time out here," the hunter asked, "when there are things that need to be done and

people who need to be cared for? This is a frivolous waste of time when there is so much to do."

The wise monk turned to the hunter and said, "Put an arrow in your bow and release it." The hunter did so. "Put in another and release it," said the monk, and the hunter did so. "And another," the monk said. Again and again, the monk instructed the hunter to string an arrow in his bow and release it.

After a short time, the hunter turned to the monk and said, "If I keep working my bow like this, it will soon break! It will be good for nothing."

"Indeed you are right," the wise old monk said to the hunter. "You know your equipment well: a bow that is too often strung tight without rest will soon break. And so it is with God's children."

Christ also understood this principle. In the Gospel (Luke 10:38–42), when Jesus visits his friends in Bethany, Martha is rushing around trying to get things done, while her sister Mary sits at Jesus' feet, simply listening. When Martha complains to Jesus, he says, in effect, "There is a time and a place for doing things, and a time and a place to sit at my feet. Mary is doing the right thing for this moment."

God created the world's natural rhythm, the turning seasons of activity and rest. In the temperate regions of our planet, the life and abundance of spring and summer grow quiet during autumn and winter. God also gave to the ancient Hebrews a weekly day of rest, called the Sabbath. Meditation is simply a way of reengaging our minds and bodies with life's natural rhythms. It is a technique for finding the Sabbath within our own hearts.

Meditation is not an esoteric practice, intended for only a few super-spiritual people. In fact, none of us can live fully or properly without it. It answers an inbuilt need for each of us, the need we each have to discover our spiritual centre: the place where our souls can catch up as we rest in the Divine Presence.

LESS STRESSED, MORE REST

Why is it that some people seem so relaxed, while others seem so wound up? Stress, and the reduction of it, is a big topic in today's society. Everywhere we turn, we hear about new ways to deal with it, from stress-management courses to Indian head massage. And yet apparently the problem persists!

The opposite of stress, is rest . . . peace . . . relaxation.

Read: Psalm 62:1–2, 5–8

These verses link the concept of rest to having security in God.

How does having God as a refuge help to relieve stress?

What do these verses teach us about trying to cope with stress alone?

Read: Matthew 11:28–30

How, according to verse 29, can you have rest for your soul?

What other stipulation is there for this rest?

What do these verses teach us about trying to cope with stress alone?

To truly relieve stress, you need God. You need quiet space to withdraw away from the rush of life, away from whatever in your life may be causing you stress.

With this understanding, you can start to live a life that does not pull you so tight that you can no longer function!

A Few Practical Ways to Relieve Stress

- Prioritise—and be willing to change priorities as things arise.
- Talk over with others you trust the things that are stressing you. Others' perspectives can help you gain perspective and new insights on your situation.
- Take frequent short breaks to step away from what you are doing.
- When you have an opportunity to have a longer break, find somewhere to go where you can completely detach from what you have been doing.
- Learn the difference between unwinding and the true rest that comes from relaxing.

4

Discovering
Our Spiritual Centre

At the center of our being
is a point of nothingness
which is untouched by illusion,
a point of pure truth,
a point or spark which belongs entirely to God
…this little point of nothingness and of absolute poverty
is the pure glory of God in us.
—*Thomas Merton*

On average, hurricanes move along at about 10 miles an hour. They are an amazing sight to behold, but they can cause enormous devastation as they pass over the earth. Their power shakes whatever is in their way and whatever is nearby. Homes are destroyed; roads and bridges crushed; cars, animals, and debris picked up and thrown. Hurricanes are not peaceful places.

So often our lives feel as though hurricanes are going through them: forces that are out our control ripping up everything we have tried to make neat and tidy, throwing it all up in the air, perhaps even destroying it. Life's hurricanes seem to come on us unexpectedly, from outside ourselves. External forces beyond our control often are to blame, but many times, our hurricanes in fact come from an imbalance somewhere within our own hearts and lives. Perhaps our work is taking up too much space in our lives; perhaps we are refusing to face something within ourselves, an area of bitterness or dishonesty or pain. Whatever caused the hurricane initially, however, once it is blowing full force, we are unable to control it or hide from it. We feel as though peace is an illusion, something longed for but impossible in the midst of so much turmoil.

But in the centre of an actual hurricane, in the eye, there *is* peace. In fact, the eye of a hurricane is one of the calmest places in the natural world. So imagine if you were able to step into the eye of a hurricane and move along with it, staying in the centre, the small circle of stillness and peace, while all around you the hurricane does what hurricanes do. The whole world would be whirling about you, but you would be sheltered in the midst of it all, in a place of perfect peace.

Although the eye of an actual hurricane is not somewhere we can ever hide, we *can* live in the eye of life's hurricanes. We do this by dwelling in our "spiritual centres," the "eyes" of our own hearts. These are the places within us where the Divine dwells. As the fourteenth-century mystic Julian of Norwich wrote, "God is the mid-point of all things, the centre on which the world turns."

This is the place of perfect peace, that which transcends the limits of our understanding, as the Apostle Paul put it (Philippians 4:7). Here at the centre of our hearts is the place where Divine peace sits, regardless of what is going on in the external world. When we make time to retreat regularly into this place, we can know and maintain our awareness of God's tranquillity even when the hurricane is blowing all around us.

This does not mean that we float through life in a state of otherworldly altered consciousness! We do not ignore the hurricane; that could be dangerous. Nor do we try to sweep the hurricane under the carpet (a tactic that is obviously doomed to failure). Instead, we live in the midst of the hurricane, filled with the peace that's found at its centre.

This Divine midpoint cannot be found by an intellectual knowledge of doctrine; instead, we find it by making an actual, experiential retreat into the Presence that lives at the centre of our inner selves. We cannot retreat to this peaceful spot without discovering our own spiritual centre points. We do this by travelling the path that takes us into the very depths of our True Selves, into the Divine image that lies within each and every one of us. When we reach it, there we will discover the peace, love, and grace of Jesus. To discover our spiritual centres is to walk the mystical path of your inner self—and arrive at the Divine One who dwells within us. Christ is the centre of all we are and all we will be.

The more often we take this path, the clearer the way becomes. Well-trod paths are easy to follow; our feet turn down them out of habit, and we reach our destination quickly. By making meditation a habit, we can learn to find our spiritual centres even in the midst of everyday life's turmoil and busyness.

Since few of us live in quiet places such as monasteries and hermitages that are isolated from the rest of the world, if we want to approach life unmoved from our spiritual centres, we must travel there constantly. Those who become well practiced at taking the path there, go so quickly and automatically that from the outside, they may seem to constantly live in that place. However, they have simply learned to slip so deeply and with such ease into the Divine presence within their spiritual centres that they seem to dwell there constantly.

From the lives and practices of those who know this way so well, we can learn to find our own paths to our quiet inner place. The "map" that leads us there has no simple instructions, such as "turn left here, right here; do this, do that." Jesus reveals himself to each person in a unique way, and in the same way, there is no single correct formula for discovering the path to our centre points.

Some of us may have stumbled on this place of peace accidentally, during some peak experience, but we may not know the way back there. We may feel as though we have to wait for God to pull us there, that we are helpless to go there on our own. In reality, however, certain practices are reliable techniques for revealing the path to our inner "eye." Not every practice is right for every person—but the following chapters will offer you basic guidelines for discovering the path that will lead you to your spiritual centre: the Presence of Christ.

Part II

Following
the Mystic Path

5

Creating a Well-Worn Path: Forming New Habits

When you begin a spiritual practice,
it is very difficult to stick with it.
But though it is difficult, persevere.
Surrender to God your sense of difficulty.
—*Brother Lawrence*

In 2011, a friend of mine who was living in breast cancer remission decided to run the London marathon to raise money for cancer research. She was not a long-distance runner; in fact, she was not a runner at all. She needed to train!

If she had decided that her training was going to start out with 26-mile runs, she would have failed repeatedly at achieving this impossible goal—and eventually, she would probably have given up. Even if she forced herself to keep running, she would in all likelihood have done herself some significant physical damage. However, my friend was sensible. She began her training with short-distance runs. As her body became accustomed to the exercise, her muscles grew stronger. Gradually, little by little, she ran longer and longer distances. And eventually, she reached the goal she had set herself: she was able to run 26 miles.

Beginning the practice of meditation needs to be approached in a similar, reasonable way. If you have never done any meditation before, you're not going to be able to sit for hours in silence. In fact, most people who are beginning meditation struggle to sit quietly for more than a few minutes. That's natural and normal. If you build up your practice slowly, little by little, you are much more likely to succeed—and you are more apt to build a permanent, ongoing habit.

Many people also struggle to commit to meditation because they feel they do not have time in their busy schedules to set aside for one more new demand. Most of us, however, even on the busiest days, find time to wash and get dressed, and we need to start seeing meditation as being just as basic and necessary to our days.

Building new habits within which meditation can thrive will make the time and effort it requires seem more manageable. I suggest the following alliterative breakdown:

- meditate momentarily
- divert daily

- withdraw weekly
- make a date monthly
- abdicate annually

Meditate Momentarily

Take small times throughout each day to stop and step back from your life. These are tiny spaces in your day, no more than five minutes at a time. See these as gifts you give to yourself, rather than as one more obligation you have to undertake. I think of them as "me moments," moments just for me.

You can do this throughout the day by stopping what you are doing, just for a few moments. If possible, close your eyes, take a few deep breaths, and relax your whole body. Breathe slowly and deeply; be aware of your breath. Let each breath carry away whatever tension you have in your body, mind, and soul. Release the stress. . . .

And then slowly return to whatever it was that you were doing.

These moments need no special place or ceremony. They can be anything from escaping to the bathroom for a few minutes and locking the door . . . to putting headphones in your ears and closing your eyes while you sit at your work desk . . . to doing what Charles and John Wesley's mother did: sitting down on a chair in the middle of the kitchen and pulling an apron over your head. (The whole Wesley family knew that if Mother was sitting with her apron over her head, she was most definitely not to be disturbed!)

Divert Daily

"To divert" means to turn in a different direction; in other words, shift your attention. You can do this by setting aside a specific space of time each day to focus on meditation. Start out with ten minutes. Work up to fifteen or twenty minutes. Eventually, you may want to expand this time to half an hour or even an hour. You may want to do it twice a day instead of just once. But start out slow! Ten minutes a day is enough to get you going.

You may want to set aside time when you first get up for meditation, to get you ready for the day—or maybe you want it to be the last thing you do before you go to bed, to quiet your mind for sleep. It may be that another time works best for your schedule—after you get the children out the door to school, for instance, or during your lunch hour at work. There's no single, right time for meditating! But once you pick a time, try to stick with it as much as possible. That way, it will become a habit, something you turn to automatically at a specific time of day.

Withdraw Weekly

Once a week, set aside time in your schedule for a longer period of time to spend sitting quietly, soaking in the Divine presence around you. A morning or an afternoon will do. Perhaps escape to some beautiful natural spot, like a forest or a shore. If you don't live somewhere you can do that conveniently, seek out instead an art gallery, a park, or a museum, somewhere quiet and serene. While there, don't think about what you have to do next; don't be constantly checking the time, worrying about when you have to resume your normal life. (Although it would be sensible to keep track of time if you need to be back for something, like picking up the children from school!) Just walk, just be, just enjoy the moment. Soak in your surroundings . . . and allow the Divine presence to soak into you.

Make a Date Monthly

Once a month, set aside an entire day to step out of your life and spend quality, focused time with God. Find a local retreat centre or monastery that's open to the public. Don't plan anything ahead of time; don't have an agenda. Simply allow yourself to be fully present in the moment throughout the entire day. Allow your awareness to be interwoven with the Divine presence. Enjoy the quiet and stillness that seeps into your inner being. Let it settle deeply into your soul and spirit.

Abdicate Annually

Once a year, make a plan to hand all your responsibilities over to someone else and go away with the express purpose of sitting with God, regaining your focus. Again, find a retreat centre or monastery that will allow you to visit over night, or find a bed-and-breakfast or hotel in a beautiful quiet surrounding. Go there and simply be.

This isn't a vacation time, nor should you think of yourself as a sightseer or tourist, someone who is in a new place to explore the surroundings. Instead, you are a pilgrim who is finding respite in an oasis of calm. Dwell in the moment. Seek God's presence.

My friend was able to successfully run the London marathon—and in an impressive time—because she disciplined herself to slowly increase her runs. You too will build habits that will allow your "meditation muscles" to grow as you commit yourself to these five practices. They will become the practical framework that allows space in your life for meditation's mystic path.

DAILY MEDITATIONS:
FOUR WEEKS OF FOCUSED PRAYER

These meditations can be part of your "divert daily" practice, to help you move from the knowledge of God's omnipresence in the world to an experience of the intimate presence of the Divine in your every day. They will help you implement biblical principles into your everyday life, so that these principles become *a way of life*, rather than *a part of your life*.

Psychologists sometimes say that if you do something for at least twenty-one days, it becomes a habit and a permanent part of your life. By doing these meditations for four weeks, you will be well on your way to making meditation a part of your everyday routine for the rest of your life.

Instructions

Find a stone that is about 1 to 2 inches round or oval. Make sure it has no points or sharp edges. Keep this stone in your pocket for the four weeks of prayer.

Why a stone?

A stone is used as a reminder to you. How often have you promised to pray for something throughout the day, only to reach the end of the day with the realisation that whatever it was had gone completely out of your mind? *A stone in your pocket is hard to ignore!* Each time you are physically reminded by touching the stone, your brain will make the connection, reminding you to pray.

A stone also represents the stability and security of the Rock of our foundation: God (Psalm 18:2; Matthew 7:25), and Jesus Christ, the cornerstone (Ephesians 2:19–22).

A stone is also unlikely to break in your pocket. And it is easily available. A smooth stone feels good to your fingers.

The Meditations

Meditation 1 each week should be done on days 1, 3, and 5 (usually Monday, Wednesday, and Friday) and Meditation 2 should be done on days 2, 4, and 6 (usually Tuesday, Thursday, and Saturday). No meditations are done on Sunday, as this day is left for gathering with others and sharing our faith.

Week 1
Meditation 1

With this stone: I will remember that God is conscious of the smallest details of His creation, of which I am a part.

Bible verses: Matthew 10:29–31

Action: Each time you are made aware of the stone, talk to God about the details of what you are doing at that moment, both routine and unusual.

Meditation 2

With this stone: I will remember that the peace of God guards my heart.

Bible verse: Philippians 4:7

Action: Each time you are made aware of the stone, close your eyes and take a deep breath in through your nose. As you breathe out slowly, say the words "the peace of God," and imagine that peace surrounding you.

Week 2

Meditation 1

With this stone: I will remember that the Lord is here to bless me.

Bible verses: Numbers 6:24–26

Action: Each time you are made aware of the stone, apply the words of this scripture to whatever you are doing at that moment.

Meditation 2

With this stone: I will remember that Christ holds all things together (and that is not my job).

Bible verse: Colossians 1:17

Action: Each time you are made aware of the stone, lay the situation you are in at the foot of the cross, remembering that it is Christ's responsibility to hold things together and not yours.

Week 3

Meditation 1

With this stone: I will remember to please the Lord.

Bible verses: Titus 2:1 and Colossians 3:17

Action: Each time you are made aware of the stone, become aware of your actions and heart attitude, and weigh them against today's scriptures.

Meditation 2

With this stone: I will remember that the integrity of my heart's desire is most important.

Bible verses: Psalm 18:20–24

Action: Each time you are made aware of the stone, take note of what you are doing and determine whether your actions honour the deepest desires that God has put into your heart.

Week 4

Meditation 1

With this stone: I will remember that I have victory through loving Jesus.

Bible verses: 1 John 5:1–5

Action: Each time you are made aware of the stone, claim the victory of Christ over your thoughts, feelings, and actions. Choose to act in a way that reflects the love of Christ

Meditation 2

With this stone: I will remember that trials and difficulties lead to my spiritual growth.

Bible verse: 1 Peter 1:4–7

Action: Each time you are made aware of the stone, focus on God's joy. Picture the circumstances you are in leading you to a deeper and greater experience of the Divine.

6

Staying on the Path: Practical Practices

*If God is to speak into your soul,
she must be completely still and quiet,
only then can he speak into her.*
—*Meister Eckhart*

Recently, I was invited to be a visiting speaker at a church. I asked the church leader if he had been focusing on a specific topic in their recent services, so that I could coordinate my talk with whatever he had been teaching. The leader told me he had been doing a series of sermons on the verse in Psalms that tells us to "be still and know that I am God" (46:10). He had looked at this verse from different angles, including the translation of the phrase as "cease striving," which he said his congregation had found easier to grasp. On another Sunday, however, he had asked the congregation to literally be still. After a period of complete silence and quietness, they had a time of interaction and feedback; almost everyone, he said, found it nearly impossible to sit and be still, even for a short period of time. I understood the church leader to be saying that at that point he felt they had come to the end of his ability to engage them with that particular verse. Perhaps I misunderstood him, but it seemed to me he was saying his congregation had tried to practise stillness, found it too hard, and so had concluded, "We can't do it. We're giving up."

This sense of defeat is one I frequently encounter as I teach workshops on meditation. Both collectively and individually, people seem to feel that stillness is an unreachable goal, one that asks something impossible of them. On this occasion, I sensed that the divinely orchestrated universe had landed me in this church on this particular Sunday morning—and needless to say, I continued their series on the subject of being still and knowing God.

In the last chapter, we talked about a five-part structure that will allow you to build meditation into your life. In this chapter, we're going to discuss what you *do* during those times, at the most basic level.

Imagine you wanted to become proficient at playing the piano. Think of these as the scales you'll need to practice before you can begin playing "Chopsticks" and "Twinkle, Twinkle, Little Star" (let alone Mozart or Beethoven).

Here are three basic foundations for the practice of meditation—and then three more things to reinforce that foundation.

Place and Setting

The first part of the structure we discussed in the last chapter—meditate momentarily—can be done anywhere, any time throughout the day. But for the next part—divert daily—you will need to find a quiet place, either inside or outside. In order for your daily time of meditation to become habitual, it helps to meditate in the same place each time. This enables your subconscious to recognise this setting as your meditation place. As you build this mental connection, you'll be amazed at how quickly and easily your brain will switch into "meditation mode" whenever you enter this spot, wherever it may be. Make sure this is a location with as few distractions as possible, somewhere you can be reasonably certain you won't be interrupted. Switch off your phone, turn off your computer!

Your designated meditation area need not be elaborate. It could be simply the corner of a room. Place a chair there and a small table, perhaps with a candle on it, some kind of visual reminder of what you are doing or something to help you focus your mind, perhaps a cross or a stone. All these reminders will also help your brain shift into its meditation mode.

Position

Obviously, God doesn't care what position your body is in when you meditate—but certain positions will help *you* focus better. Here are some suggestions:

- Sit in a comfortable position—but not so comfortable that you're likely to fall asleep. Sitting cross-legged on the floor is a good position, and so is kneeling with your feet pointing out behind you. (Your feet muscles may need to get used to this one, or you may wish to purchase a kneeling stool.) In either case, make sure your back is straight. You can also sit in a chair with your back straight, again making sure you are not so comfortable you will fall asleep. You can either sit cross-legged in the chair or place your legs straight in front of you, with both feet flat on the floor.

- Rest your hands in front of you, on your thighs or knees. The positioning of your hands can also help focus your thoughts. For example, I often start my meditation with my hands out over my knees with palms facing down. I do this as a sign that I am simply becoming still and centring myself. Then I often move my hands so that my palms are facing upward. This helps me to picture opening myself to the Divine presence. I also sometimes use a Zen hand position, forming a circle with my thumb tips touching and my fingertips resting upon each other. This helps me focus on Divine eternity and my connection with that eternal reality.

These positions can help you focus mentally—but there is no right or wrong position while meditating!

Breathing

Your breathing is important, whether you are meditating momentarily, taking a tiny "me moment" in the midst of your busy day, or spending an entire day in meditation. Correct breathing will help you relax more deeply and concentrate more precisely. There's nothing worse than spending your entire meditation time constantly interrupted by yawning!

Breathing may seem like the most obvious and basic of activities, the sort of thing you don't need to think about in order to do. But stop for a moment and focus on your breathing pattern; take a few deep breaths. Inhale, exhale. Inhale, exhale. Pay attention. You will notice, if you are not out of breath, that your breathing pattern consists of more than just in-and-out, in-and-out; there is a natural pause between each exhalation and the next inhalation.

I once participated in a training day with St. John's Ambulance crew. They taught us many things—like how to do resuscitation while reciting "Nelly the elephant" in our heads! The instructor also described the process of breathing in a way I have used regularly in teaching meditation and relaxation ever since. She said that when we breathe in, we take in everything that is around us; then our lungs separate everything we need from the air and we breathe out everything we don't need. In the pause between exhalation and inhalation, the body sends all the useful parts of the breath into the blood stream. This moment of rest, she said, is where we gain the fullness of life.

This is what happens during meditation, on the spiritual and psychological levels as much as the physical. We are created as body, soul, and mind, all linked together, and through breathing, we make real the unity of our being.

The best way to breathe during meditation is to draw in air deeply through your nose. Do not over do it—you are not trying to hold your breath or hyperventilate—but fill your lungs to a good capacity. When you breathe out (it doesn't really matter if you breath out through your nose or mouth), do it gradually, slowly enough that you cannot hear the breath coming out of you. Then let the natural rest in your breathing pattern sit for as long as it needs to before you breathe in again.

By focusing on your breath, you bring your mind back from all the external things that have been occupying it. You connect to the here and now. This is the moment where God wants to meet you, at the most basic and intimate level of your breath.

ONE-MINUTE MEDITATION

Focus your attention on your breathing. Take four long, deep breaths, being sure to rest between each. The rest is usually about half the length of the in-and-out parts, so try to take around five to six seconds to breathe in fully, five to six seconds to breathe out, and two to three seconds to rest or pause between exhalation and inhalation. This will add up to about fifteen seconds per cycle, around four cycles per minute.

This exercise can be done at any time anywhere. You don't need to close your eyes, although if you are able to, do so. Repeat the exercise to fill whatever space of time you have free to meditate. If you do the exercise about once an hour or every couple of hours every day, you will soon begin to feel a greater sense of inner peace and calm. You might want to imagine that as you inhale, you are drawing in the Holy Spirit; as you exhale, you are surrendering your ego, letting go of all that comes between you and the Divine.

These are the three most basic and practical practices that will guide you on the mystic path: place, position, and breath. With these three, you are ready to set out on your journey. But I want to also share with you three more things I find helpful.

Atmosphere

Creating an atmosphere—combining sense stimuli—offers your brain additional triggers that will allow you to achieve a quiet, focused state of mind quickly and easily. There really are no rights and wrongs here; create an atmosphere that works for you, using the elements of sound, scent, and spirit.

music

I find that gentle music playing softly helps my mental focus. My concentration drifts naturally in and out of the music, and I resist mental distractions more easily, allowing me to more readily sense the Divine presence and the spiritual realm. Personally, I like indigenous music, from Celtic to Tibetan flute; I have created a playlist on my iPod of music I find conducive for meditation. You may prefer classical music or traditional worship music, jazz or bluegrass, New Age or simply recorded nature sounds. What's important is that the music not be vocal, so that your concentration is not broken by the temptation to sing along with the words.

incense

Today, we often connect incense with either hippies or "high church" forms of worship—but incense has drawn people's attention to God for thousands of years. The ancient Israelites used incense in their worship, and many other spiritual traditions do so as well. Although we often think with a dualistic perspective, perceiving our senses and our souls as operating in separate realms, in fact, God can work through our senses to reach our souls, and we can use our physical senses to help us come into the Divine presence.

Aromas are a good way to fill a meditation space, providing a sensual meditation trigger. Particular aromas can aid concentration in different ways. I use essential oil burners—but I prefer to burn incense, because I can both see and smell the smoke rising from the burner and filling the room. I see the Spirit's presence and I breathe in the sweet aroma of the Divine.

Some years ago, I was involved in putting on a youth event in the local cathedral of the village where we lived at the time. We removed all the pews and installed flashing lights and large speakers for the DJ. On the evening of the event, the place was hazy from the smoke machine on the stage, and the thousands of young people who came sensed the Divine presence in a way in which many of them had never done before. The smoke machine provided a modern version of incense.

In the weeks leading up to the event, however, I had experienced the more traditional version, every morning when I went to the cathedral to pray before it was open to public. In those quiet, early-morning moments, I shared the cathedral with one other person: the incense swinger. As I walked around the cathedral praying, seeking the Divine presence, the incense swinger would also be walking around the cathedral, gently swinging his incense burner on its long chains. As I prayed, I would gradually become more and more engulfed in smoke.

On the night of the event, as I watched the smoke pour across the stage, my mind was drawn back to those smoky, scented mornings. My physical senses instantly made the connection, and the sight of smoke drew me into an awareness of the Divine there in the cathedral.

invocation

When we invoke the Spirit, we ask the Divine to be present with us. This is particular to spiritual meditation, and even more particular to Christ-centred meditation. As you meditate, you call out to God, asking that the Divine Spirit be with you, inhabiting each element of the atmosphere.

During meditation, you are not asking God to do anything for you aside from being present. You are not seeking Divine blessing for yourself; you are not interceding on behalf of others, lifting up their problems to God. You are not asking God to reveal anything to you or to change you. You are simply asking that God come and sit with you, rest with you, and guide your heart and mind. You are asking only that God fill this present moment of space and time.

Focus

I am easily distracted. I once had a spiritual director who always placed my chair so that my back would be toward the window whenever we met; otherwise, she had learned my attention would be drawn to something outside rather than whatever was going on inside the room.

The same sort of thing can distract us from meditation. With practice, we get better at focusing anywhere, regardless of noise and visual distractions, but especially as we're starting out in our practice, we need to find places where there are fewer things to pull our attention away from our meditation. Even in a bare, empty cell, however, our busy minds can offer their own sort of distractions.

Having an external focal point can help you maintain your inner focus. This could be a lit candle, a cross, a stone in your hand, an icon, or a photograph. As your physical senses focus on this specific thing, your mind becomes more focused as well, and mental distractions are less frequent.

Focal points do not have to rely on your physical senses, however; alternatively, you could meditate with your eyes closed, focusing on an internal picture. This might be a particular place where you have experienced Divine peace in the past, such as the beach or a spot in the forest or a church sanctuary. I often draw my mind's eye to a particular spot on the Holy Island of Lindisfarne. You might imagine the sound of waves lapping on the shore or the wind in the tree branches. With the power of your memory and your imagination (both God-given abilities), you can leave your actual location, wherever that is, and rest your mind in a quiet place far from distractions.

Thoughts

All these techniques will help you meditate. But all meditation must confront what is sometimes called the monkey mind: the constant mental chatter that never stops. How can we have peace when our brains are so relentlessly *busy*?

Many times people try to tackle this dilemma with sheer determination and will power. But this is a bit like trying to empty a bath full of pink water by pouring blue water into it: the tub just gets fuller and fuller. When we try to consciously stop thinking, this very act is a thought; now we are thinking about not thinking, and our brains are busier than ever! We need to take the plug out of the bathtub and let the water run out. We do this by letting our thoughts chatter on, while we disengage from them. We step aside and simply watch their stream.

Imagine you are standing on a riverbank, gazing at things that float by you on the river. You observe these things without trying to either grab hold of them or push them away. During meditation, your thoughts are the objects floating on the river. When you realise you have become engaged with one of them, simply acknowledge the fact and then let the thought drift on its way again. Let it float away from you on the river as you return your focus to meditation.

Your monkey mind is stubborn and incorrigible. You may wonder if it will ever learn to quiet down. But be patient with yourself. When you first start this practice, you may feel as though you are wasting your time because you spend the entire period of meditation letting go of the thoughts that keep engaging your attention. But as you get more practiced, the time your thoughts take to run to an end will become less and less, until it only takes a very short time.

Brother Lawrence, a seventeenth-century monk who was adept at meditating, said:

> When your thoughts wander (as they will), don't worry about it, since worry will only distract you further. Bring yourself back to silence, to tranquillity.

> You are not the only one who is troubled with wandering thoughts during times of prayer. Our minds scatter their arrows every which way, here and there, without a target. In the end, however, you can choose to carry all of them to God. (*Brother Lawrence: A Christian Zen Master*, Anamchara Books, 2010)

EXERCISES

Sit in a position where your lungs are not cramped up (no slouching), either on a chair, your bed, or on the floor. If on the floor, then either kneel with your toes stretched out behind you (this may take some muscle-stretching practice) or sit crossed-legged. However you sit, place your hands on your thighs or knees with your palms upward in an expression of release. Close your eyes.

Breathe in deeply through your nose (you will get the most oxygen possible by breathing in through your nose rather than your mouth), so that your lungs fill to a point where you can feel them pull. Breathe out again (either through your nose or mouth, it doesn't matter) slowly, so that you cannot hear the breath leaving your body. When you have exhaled all of your breath, rest for two to four seconds before you breathe in again. Do this for three or four breaths. Then breathe in through your nose until your chest starts to expand and your head will probably lift (this inhalation should be slightly less deep than the first set of breaths). Breathe out again slowly (this time it does not matter if you can hear your breath), and then rest again for two to four seconds before breathing in again. Do this for three or four breaths. Then breathe slowly at a lung capacity that feels comfortable for five or six breaths. Open your eyes and slowly get up—or move into the following exercise that will help you relax.

Sit or lie back in a comfortable position. Close your eyes or simply gaze at something with your eyes focused (do not let your eyes wander). Allow a feeling of relaxation to flow from the top of your head through to the front of your forehead. Concentrate on releasing the tension that may be in your head. Each time you breathe out, visualise the tension leaving your body. Let the feeling of relaxation flow into the muscles in your face, feel it flowing through the small muscles around your eyes and nose, feel it as it slips around your jaw bone, and continue to breathe away the tension as you exhale. Allow the feeling to flow down your neck and across your shoulders, down your upper arms, lower arms, running out through your fingertips, all the while breathing out the tension. With each breath you take, allow the tension of the day to ebb away like the tide slowly receding from the shore. Visualise the tide and hear the sound growing further and further away. Allow the tensions of the day to ride away on the water. Continue the flow of relaxation down your body, through every muscle; allow your chest to relax, allow your stomach to relax, and let the relaxation flow down your legs and out through your toes in the same way it flowed down your arms and out through your fingers. Now let the flow run down from the back of your head, down your spine, like a gentle waterfall washing away the tension of the day. Let it run off of your spine and into your buttocks and the back of your legs, gently ebbing away through your heels.

If you want, you can move back into the first exercise now, to increase your sense of relaxation.

7

Travelling Deeper: Meditating on Scripture

Some people like to read
so many [Bible] chapters every day.
I would not dissuade them from the practice,
but I would rather lay my soul asoak
in half a dozen verses all day
than rinse my hand in several chapters.
Oh, to be bathed in a text of Scripture,
and to let it be sucked up in your very soul,
till it saturates your heart!
—*Charles Haddon Spurgeon*

These basic practices we discussed in the last two chapters will get you on the mystic path. Now it is up to you to travel further along this way. A variety of practices will make the path clearer to you. One of the most important for those of us who follow Christ is using scripture as a focal point for our meditation.

We often have a strange view of the Bible. Many times we seem to think that because somewhere along the line someone divided scripture into chapters and verses, those divisions were intended by God. As a result, we often assume we can read a small section of the Bible each day and be done with it. We don't have this view of other books; we wouldn't pick up a novel and say, "Right, today I will read the second paragraph of page 46 and then the last two paragraphs on page 215." And yet we do this with the Bible. Context is important. Comprehending the entire picture is necessary if we want to have a better intellectual understanding. We are rational beings, and we are meant to use our minds as we engage with our faith. However, intellectual knowledge is not the goal of mediation.

To meditate upon scripture is not to read the Bible for information; instead, it is to nourish yourself with words that are living and dynamic, to allow them to soak deep into your imagination and into your unconscious mind. This is an ancient practice, one that Saint Benedict called Lectio Divina (divine reading).

The practice of Lectio Divina can be separated into five parts: read, reflect, respond, rest, relate.

Read
Set aside time each day to read scripture, but during this time don't be concerned about volume. In other words, don't say to yourself, "Today I will read three chapters"—

or two chapters or even one chapter. Instead, slowly begin reading a scripture passage, savouring each word and phrase. Read until you notice a word or phrase that jumps out at you. This word or phrase will touch something in you; it will resonate with you or attract you in some way. It may even disturb you. When this happens, don't read any further. Read and reread the same sentence or verse. Come back to it again on the following day, and maybe even for several days. Stay with it.

Reflect

Think about what this passage is saying to you. Ponder the word or phrase. Be like Mary who treasured God's words to her and pondered them in her heart (Luke 2:19). Let the scripture word or phrase sink deeper and deeper, through all the layers of your thoughts. Allow God to speak to you through it. Listen for what this scripture says to you within the circumstances of your current life. Don't think in abstracts or concern yourself with doctrine and theology. (There is a time and place for that, but this is not it.) What gifts does this passage offer you? What insights rise to the surface of your heart? What does it demand of you?

Respond

The Benedictines refer to this step as *oratio*: prayer. In other words, express what is within your heart in words of thanksgiving . . . or petition; praise . . . or lament.

Be honest with God. You may want to respond aloud, or you may want to speak silently to God within your mind. You might want to write down your thoughts. If you linger with the same Bible passage for several days, recording your responses each day in a journal, when you look back you may be surprised how many different things came out of your heart in response to the same word or phrase.

Rest

At the end of your meditation, let go of all your thoughts. Surrender even the words themselves upon which you have been meditating. Allow yourself to rest silently in God's love and peace. A mother holding her sleeping baby doesn't need to speak to communicate her love, nor do lovers need to fill every moment with chatter in order to commune with each other. This is the same sort of moment between you and God, a moment of intimacy and total trust.

Relate

It is no good reading the Bible, even if God speaks to you through it, if you do not relate it to the way you live your life. We're not talking here about applying religious rules to your life or trying to "be good." Instead, take the particular passage of scripture with you throughout the day. Allow it to continue to work in your mind and heart. When you take a "me moment," think back to the word or phrase.

See how it applies to the daily circumstances of your life. Allow it to weave through the hours of your everyday life.

Don't think of these five things as items to be checked off on a list each time you sit down to practise Lectio Divina. You won't necessarily move through each of them in the same order every time. Allow yourself freedom. The only goal is to move into the still, peaceful place where you can hear God's Word speak lovingly to your heart—and where you can respond.

Lectio Divina should be a spontaneous movement from the Word into silence and back into the Word. Allow the Word to merge with your inmost thoughts. Dwell with it throughout your day. Let it lead you again and again into God's quiet presence.

LECTIO DIVINA BIBLE READINGS

The following Bible readings will take you through twelve weeks of Lectio Divina.

I am God's child.
John 1:12

I am known by Jesus.
John 10:14

The Spirit of God is in me.
John 14:16

Nothing can stop God's love.
Romans 8:38–39

I am wonderful.
Psalm 139:14

I am saved and called; I belong to God.
Isaiah 43:1

God sings love songs over me.
Zephaniah 3:17

I am made by God to do good things.
Ephesians 2:10

I am saved through God's work, not mine.
Titus 3:4–5

I need not be anxious; I can be filled with peace.
Philippians 4:6–7

I need to guard my heart.
Proverbs 4:23

I can filter my life through these eight layers.
Philippians 4:8

8

The Ever-Present Path: Practising the Presence of God

My soul has a habitual,
silent, secret conversation with God.
—*Brother Lawrence*

In the seventeenth century, a French Carmelite monk named Brother Lawrence discovered he could live with a constant sense of God's presence while immersed in his work in the monastery kitchen. A humble and un-educated man, he nevertheless became famous, not for his teaching or writing, but simply for his way of liv-ing. He had such serenity and joy that others wanted to know his secret. He even attracted the attention of an important church leader, who sent an envoy, an abbe, to interview Brother Lawrence. After their meeting, the abbe wrote down Brother Lawrence's responses to his questions, and this record, along with a few notes and a handful of letters, were all Brother Lawrence left behind when he died at the age of eighty. These brief paragraphs were put together and became *The Practice of the Presence of God*, a small inspirational book that has been read by thousands over the past three hundred years. Today, it continues to offer practical help to those of us seeking to follow the mystic path of meditation.

Brother Lawrence taught that having a true understanding of the Divine existence means your mind can be as fully focused on God while you do your daily work, just as much as it would be if you were praying in church. He said:

> We should not set aside our prayer time as being different from the other hours in the day. If we do, we tend to assume that we need not cling as tightly to God in the active moments of our day, when we are busy with daily concerns. The reality is just the opposite. Times devoted to prayer may have their proper place in our lives—but we need to pay equally close attention to God's presence at all times, no matter what we are doing.

> I see no difference between set times of prayer and the rest of my life. My Superior here at the monastery tells me to go to my cell to pray at certain times of the day, so I do—but I don't need those times to maintain my prayer life. No matter how busy I am, I'm always focused on God. Life

no longer distracts me. Instead, each task, no matter how small, is like a prayer bead that focuses my attention on God. (*Brother Lawrence: A Christian Zen Master*, Anamchara Books, 2011)

Once Brother Lawrence had begun the day with a time of quiet, he said when he began the work he had to do that day, he would say to God, "O my God, since You are with me, and I must now, in obedience to You, apply my mind to these outward things, I beseech You to grant me the grace to continue in Your presence; and to this end, receive all my works, and possess all my affections." Notice that Brother Lawrence accepted that he was where God wanted him to be, at least for the day ahead, and thus he could think of his practical work as being an assignment from God. He could then carry on with that work, all the while continuing his familiar conversation with God, asking for Divine grace and offering up all his actions to God. He lived within his busy life absorbed in the presence of God.

Meister Eckhart, another great Christian mystic, wrote three or four hundred years earlier:

Some people prefer solitude. They say their peace of mind depends on this. Others say they would be better off in church. If you do well, you do well wherever you are. If you fail, you fail wherever you are. Your surroundings don't matter. God is with you everywhere—in the market place as well as in seclusion or in the church. If you look for nothing but God, nothing or no one can disturb you. God is not distracted by a multitude of things. Nor can we be.

In a similar vein, Evelyn Underhill, the twentieth-century author best known for her writings on mysticism, wrote:

> Never think that because God has given you many things to do for him—pressing routine jobs; a life full up with duties and demands of a very particular sort—that all these need separate you from communion with him. God is always coming to you in the sacrament of the present moment [whatever you are doing]. Meet and receive him there with gratitude in that sacrament; however unexpected its outward form may be.

This idea of committing all that we do to God, and thereby finding God's presence in ordinary life, is a much older teaching than that explained by Evelyn Underhill, Brother Lawrence, or even Meister Eckhart. It goes back to the Apostle Paul who wrote in his letter to the Colossian church, "whatever you do, whether in word or deed, do it all in the name of Jesus, giving thanks to God the Father through him." (3:17 NIV), and this in turn reflected Paul's Hebraic understanding of still more ancient religious traditions.

So we can see that daily, moment-by-moment meditation is no new-fangled, New Age idea. We have always been called to find God in all things, in all places, at all times. Meditation interweaves with our entire life. Spiritual retreats and church time are good and necessary—but dwelling in the presence of God is a far wider, deeper practice.

MINDFULNESS

Mindfulness is the practice of meditation while being active in everyday life. To become mindful is to open the eyes of your heart—or your mind's eye—to the things going on around you and within you as you live life. In doing this, in becoming proficient in this practice, we start to see the Spirit of God in all things and on all occasions, whether at home (even when doing household chores), out in the wonder of creation, walking down the street, or sitting in front of a computer working.

In the words of a prayer by David Adam from his book *The Eye of the Eagle*:

Open my eyes that I may see the Presence that is all about me.
Open my ears that I may hear the voice that is quiet but ever near.
Open my heart that I may feel the love of my God, close and real.
Open each sense, make me aware of the power and peace always there.

Exercise

Begin your practice of mindfulness by feeling the beat of your heart. If you are walking, keep pace with the rhythm of your heartbeat. Try not to speed up as you walk. Then concentrate on your breathing, as explained in earlier chapters.

Now use the words of Adam's prayer to help you focus your mind. Start to notice the things around you. If you are outside, or can see the outside world through a window, take in the movement of nature. Watch the flight of birds, listen for their song. See the trees swaying in the wind or standing still in perfect peace. If people are around you, look at them. See them as unique individuals. Repeat David Adam's words again (or something similar) as a prayer as you watch. Try to sense— to see with the eye of your heart—the presence of God within and around all things.

Mindfulness While Cleaning House

The term "cleaning house" has a literal meaning (cleaning up your actual house), as well as a figurative one (getting rid of emotional clutter, letting go of things that no longer serve you)—and both can be great stress relievers. Actual clutter in your physical world can cause you stress, so cleaning house as a mindfulness exercise brings benefits on many levels.

First, think of housecleaning as an exercise in self-understanding and stress relief, rather than as a chore. Then, as you clean, focus on what you are doing as you are doing it—and nothing else. Feel the warm, soapy water on your hands as you wash dishes; experience the vibrations of the vacuum cleaner as you push it back and forth across the floor; enjoy the warmth of the laundry as you fold it; feel the freedom of letting go of unneeded objects as you put them in the donations bag. I also recommend adding music to the equation. Don't try to manufacture "spiritual" thoughts. Simply be present to the movements of your body. Offer them to God.

The best spiritual practice I have found
is simply my ordinary, everyday work.
When I do my work for God,
rather than to impress others,
my work brings me to God.

If I so much as pick up something
that's dropped on the ground,
I find joy in doing it for God.
—Brother Lawrence

Mantras

Brother Lawrence understood that the practice of the presence of God is not easy, especially at first. He said:

DAVID COLE

Don't be surprised if at first you fail to keep your focus on God. Don't give up. After a while, turning your thoughts toward God will become a habit. This habit will naturally lead to a certain way of acting. The habit will carry you along, effortlessly and delightfully.

And he added, "Go about your life without anxiety, and no matter how many times your mind wanders from God, bring it back gently and peacefully." Brother Lawrence brought his mind back to its focus on God by repeating a few short words throughout the day: "Make me according to Your heart, God. Make my thoughts Yours."

You may find that a prayer phrase like this will draw your mind and heart's focus back to God. However, even Brother Lawrence's short prayer may be too long for your busy life. If that's the case, a single word can become an automatic prayer that will restore your sense of God's presence.

For hundreds, perhaps even thousands of years, people have been using what meditators call a "mantra" to help focus their thoughts and hearts. A mantra is simply repeating a single word or short phrase to enable you to maintain your focus. Some Christians are uneasy with this concept, thinking that it is a Hindu practice that is contrary to Christ-centred faith. The term "mantra" does originate within Hinduism, but it is simply a word, like meditation or mysticism, one that can be applied usefully to any faith or practice. The word *mantra* is a Sanskrit word that literally meant "an instrument of thought": in other words, a tool that helped mental clarity. In modern usage, "mantra" refers simply to a sound, syllable, word, or short sentence that's used to aid meditative focus. If you're uncomfortable with the word, however, perhaps you might like to use the term "monologistic prayer," which means simply "one-word prayer."

Again, mantras are nothing new; short, ongoing prayers like this have been used in Christ-centred meditation for hundreds of years. The earliest recorded example comes from John Cassian in the late fourth century, who suggested using the words from the beginning of Psalm 69—*Save me, O God; for the waters are come in unto my soul*—as a repeated prayer throughout the day; we can logically assume that this was already a well-used practice during Cassian's day. Later, in the fifth century, Benedict used similar words in his Divine Office (which is still used today). Further on in our spiritual heritage, in the fourteenth century, the unknown author of the great mystical work *The Cloud of Unknowing* wrote that a one-word prayer "pierces heaven far more swiftly than a whole set of mumbled psalms . . . just as someone in a burning building would simply shout 'help' or 'fire' from the depths of their being." The author suggested that repeating a single word such as "God" or "Love" can encompass all that we mean: "the way to pray is that which compresses your whole being in the simplicity of one syllable." In the twentieth century, John Main, a Benedictine monk who taught mantra prayer, suggested the simple prayer "Come, Lord," which in Aramaic (the language Jesus spoke) is a single word: *Maranatha*.

This simple word becomes habitual the more often you repeat it. To aid you in your concentration, you may repeat the word out loud in monotone syllables—"MA-RA-NA-THA"—two or three times in a row, several times throughout your day. Practice saying this each morning as you get out of bed, for example, and each night before you sleep . . . and then as you begin any new activity, inviting the Divine presence into what you do. The use of this simple word at the start and during all things that you do will ensure that you are continually aware of the Divine presence.

Another mantra I have found helpful is the phrase from John's Gospel, chapter 3, verse 30: "He must become greater, I must become less." This short phrase, continually repeated through your day, will inevitably focus you more on the Divine presence, while you let go of your selfish ego.

Psychologists know that our attitudes are shaped by our thoughts. So you might want to affirm that you believe the Divine presence is with you by saying so. Follow the example of Francis of Assisi, who prayed throughout his day, "Here I am Lord, here you are Lord, here we are together"—or you could simply pray, "You are here, Lord." Practise saying this silently in your mind as well as out loud. Create triggers throughout your day that will remind you to make this affirmation. Say it as you click "open" on your e-mail inbox—as you get in your car or on the train or bus to go to work—as you walk through the door at your workplace—as you return home at the end of the day. Each time you move from one activity or place to another, repeat again: "You are here, Lord."

Other Meditation Techniques

Some people may find a visual image works better for them than a spoken work as a tool for focusing their minds. This is the purpose of icons, used most often in Eastern Orthodox churches, but mental imagery can also help you practise the presence of God. Picture Jesus beside you, with you, as you go through your day. Concentrate on his presence there with you; feel him, know him there. Perhaps more than any practice, this will help shape the way you act throughout the day. Jesus is not your imaginary friend, but there's nothing wrong with using the powers of your imagination to help you grasp spiritual reality and practise the presence of God.

A string of beads can be another useful meditation tool. The rosary is probably the form of prayer beads most familiar to many Christians, but other faiths also use prayer beads, and all these can be adapted for your individual practice. The beads are used with a mantra, as a tactile tool for focusing the mind, something that can be done anywhere any time.

I usually wear a mala bead bracelet, a string of twenty-seven small reddish beads with a large bead where the string joins. Mala beads are always strung in multiples of three, no matter how long they are, which makes them lend themselves to easy mantras based on the names of a Triune God; for example, as I pass the beads through my fingers, I often repeat, "Abba . . . Ruach . . . M'shiach": the Hebrew words for Father, Spirit, and Messiah. Or I might pronounce the three syllables of YHWH: "Je-Ho-Vh." I repeat the three words or syllables until I reach the large bead again, from where I started, at which point I may say something like, "Christ is my Rabbi, I will follow him." I may go round and round the bracelet numerous times, and when I have finished passing the beads through my fingers, I simply slip the bracelet back onto my wrist.

MEDITATION MOMENTS

We all have brief moments in our lives where we have to stop. We can choose to use these moments to gain or maintain a sense of inner calm.

Red Lights

Every day, most of us who drive will at some point need to stop at a red light. This is a perfect opportunity to grab a meditation moment!

Once you have come to a stop, take two or three slow deep breaths in and out through your nose.

Look at the red light.

Focus on it.

Breathe deeply.

Let all thoughts drift out of your mind.

Smile. Thank God for this opportunity that life has given you to be able to just take a moment to stop.

As the light changes from red to green, allow the sense of stillness to continue within you. Take the sense of calm with you as you continue to drive . . . until you get to the next red light, where you get to do it all again!

In a Lift

Standing in a lift, travelling between floors, is another opportunity to grab a meditation moment.

When you step into the lift, stand still and take two or three slow deep breaths in and out though your nose. As the lift travels either up or down, feel its movement; feel it transport you from one place to another. If you are going up, imagine yourself being lifted above the things in your life that worry you. If you are going down, imagine yourself going deeper into a sense of calm.

Breathe slowly and deeply as the lift takes you to the floor where you need to leave it. As you step out of the lift, smile and feel a sense of gratitude for this small, quiet moment.

At a Bus Stop or Train Station

Waiting for a bus or a train is one more opportunity to grab a meditation moment.

Sit or stand still, and take two or three slow, deep breaths in and out though your nose.

Allow your body to relax.

Let all thoughts drift away from your mind.

Let your ears fill with the sounds of traffic and people.

What other sounds can you hear? Birds? Dogs? Rain?

Breathe slowly and deeply as you listen. As you get onto your bus or train, smile and thank God for this opportunity to just take a moment to stop.

On a Bus or Train

Riding public transportation, whether for your morning commute to work or for some other reason, is yet another good opportunity to grab a meditation moment.

Sit or stand still and take two or three slow deep breaths in and out though your nose.

Feel the movement of the bus or train.

Allow the sense of movement to be your focus.

Hear the sounds made by the wheels.

Breathe slowly and deeply as you sit or stand and listen and feel the sense of movement.

As you get off at your destination, smile and thank God for this opportunity to step out of your busy life for a moment.

Other Opportunities

Life is filled with moments when we have to wait. In our hurry-up world, we often regard these moments as sources of frustration. Instead, we can choose to claim these as "me moments," occasions for momentary meditation. Each life has its own share of these occasions when we are asked to stop and wait. Here are just a few examples:

- waiting on hold for a telephone call
- waiting for a program to load on the computer
- waiting at the mechanic for our car to be repaired
- waiting in line at an office or store
- waiting in the doctor's waiting room

The Tabernacle of God

The meditation practices we have discussed so far in this chapter have all focused on techniques that will help you to interweave meditation throughout your daily life, bringing the mystic awareness of God's presence to the ordinary activities and responsibilities that occupy you throughout the day. These are the "me moments" we discussed in chapter 5. Another equally important meditation technique, however, is the practice of "tabernacling" with God, making times when you consciously withdraw from the rest of life. These are the other four levels of practice described in chapter 5: "divert daily," "withdraw weekly," "make a date monthly," and "abdicate annually."

The ancient Hebrew scriptures describe the tabernacle—the *mishkan*, in Hebrew—the sacred tent that God told Moses to build to house the Divine presence while the Israelites were in the wilderness. Mishkan means "dwelling," and the tabernacle was a physical space where the Divine presence could meet with the people. To be in the Divine presence was to be in the tabernacle, and to be in the tabernacle was to be in the Divine presence. Unlike the temple, which was built later in Jewish history, the tabernacle was a portable sanctuary.

When Jesus came to the Earth around 2,000 years ago, the Apostle John tells us that he "made his dwelling among us" (1:14). Although John wrote in Greek, and so the word he used was *skenoo*, it is equivalent to the He-brew *mishkan*. John tells us that Jesus tabernacled with us: he dwelt with us, he pitched his tent in our midst. This was far more than a casual visit; he became involved with our living. He created a sanctuary, a place of safety for us, where we could be with God's presence.

In our own lives, "tabernacles" are the places we seek out where we can truly discover who we are, places where we encounter the Divine image within us. In practical terms, this takes planning; these occasions seldom happen otherwise.

You may start out with a weekly, monthly, and yearly plan, as outlined in chapter 5, but as your medi-tation muscles become stronger, you can build onto this and find predictable brief tabernacle moments within every day. For example, if your job allows for employees to take a cigarette break, you might stand outside dwelling with God, simply focusing on the Di-vine presence for a few moments. Your car might be your tabernacle, where you use music and prayer to focus your thoughts on God as you drive to and from work. If you ride the bus or train, you might find that headphones allow you to create tabernacle moments even while surrounded by other passengers. Your daily shower can even be a tabernacle moment.

These moments of meditation are not for reading or study (certainly not when in the shower!) or even for active prayer. Instead, tabernacle moments are more like when we sit quietly on the sofa with someone we love. We don't need to always be speaking, we don't always need to even be physically touching: simply dwelling in the same place with this beloved person can be a deep comfort. Do this with God. Enter the Divine tabernacle. Pitch a tent where you can dwell in God's presence—even if it's just an apron thrown over your face whenever life gets to be too much to handle!

As these practices become habit, the mystic path to your spiritual centre will become easier to find. The more you practise, the faster you will find the path, and the shorter will be the journey along it to the centre . . . where you can rest in the peace and calm of the Divine presence.

9

Knowing God: Meditating on the Divine Character

Magnify the Lord with me.
Let us lift up God's Name together.
—*Psalm 34:3*

Whether we believe in God or not, most of us think we know God's name. We have grown up hearing the word "God," and we take for granted that we know what we mean when we say it. But as the great Christian mystics make clear down through the centuries, whatever concepts of God we have are inadequate. If we simply maintain that God is only who we *think* God is, then we have put limits on the Divine character, and on ourselves as well. To meditate upon the character of God—the Divine identity—is to open ourselves to a greater and deeper understanding of who God is. In the process, we allow ourselves to be changed.

The Apostle Paul went through this process. He was born Saul and had been brought up as a devout Jew. As someone who studied the scriptures, he was certain he knew who God was—and because of his limited understanding of the Divine character, he was extremely hard on the new sect that called themselves followers of Jesus Christ. In fact, Saul's mindset was a lot like the one that was prevalent during the Spanish Inquisition: he tortured and killed the followers of the Way (as they were called at the time). And then Saul had an encounter with God that was far beyond his experience. On the road to Damascus, God stopped him in his tracks.

Saul had always known who God was, or at least he thought he did. After all, he was an intelligent and religious man who had been trained by the best rabbis of the time. And yet, as he fell on the ground, blinded by the Divine light, he asked what could be the most important question any of us can ask: "Who are you, Lord?" Up until then, Saul had had a fixed idea in his head of who God was—but now he was confronted by the Divine reality. He learned something new about God, something that changed and transcended his rigid view of God. Something that transformed his life.

Imagine the history of the church if instead, Saul had said, "No, I already know who God is. I know what God is like. I know how God works. This vision does not fit in with my ideas about God—and so I refuse to accept it! I will maintain the view of God I learned from the best spiritual teachers, and it will not change."

Few of us are likely to have a Road-to-Damascus sort of experience, where God reaches down and violently interrupts our comfortable lives. We can, however, choose through meditation's mystic path to seek the same light that blinded Saul and transformed him into Paul. To meditate upon the Divine character is to open ourselves to this experience. Though it is likely to be a far less dramatic process than the one Paul experienced, it may nonetheless be just as earth shaking to our perspectives on ourselves and our relationship to God.

Practising the Character of God

As we go about our lives, we often tend to be spiritual and psychological chameleons: we automatically blend in with the society around us. Without ever making a conscious decision, we absorb values and attitudes that are far different from God's character. We shouldn't beat ourselves up for doing this; it's simply a natural human tendency, a part of our genetic makeup. But it can hide the Divine character that lives within us. Meditation techniques can be practical tools for counteracting this.

As a conscious act, in your "tabernacle moments" invite the Holy Spirit to show you what is dominating your nature at that moment. It may be panic, as you worry about a loved one's health, or how a conflict will turn out, or why you have to go and see your boss at the end of the day; it may be anger or resentment, because someone has hurt you or treated you unfairly; it may be greed, because you have absorbed the flow of consumerism and advertising that tells you constantly that you need more, more, more; it may be pride, as the ego part of you takes control, preoccupied with what others think of your appearance, your job performance, your skills and talents.

Once you have allowed the Holy Spirit to show you what is dominating your being at that moment, you must first be open enough to acknowledge and accept it—and then you can focus on whatever the opposite tendency would be. The opposite of panic would be calm; the opposite of anger and resentment could be love; the opposite of greed would be generosity; the opposite of pride would be humility. Now you can carry your meditation out into the active world and *practise* the opposite qualities. This is practising the character of God in your life. This practice will not only help you be more at peace as you go through life, but it will also help you to get to know God's character still more deeply. And the more you practise God's character, the more it will become yours as well.

When I was young my parents sent me to piano lessons. I didn't get very far because I didn't practise all that much. My sister, however, started lessons at the same time but practised regularly and kept with it; today, she plays the piano very well. When I took driving lessons, however, I applied myself more than I had to piano lessons. At the beginning, I wasn't a very good driver. I was driving a car with manual gears, and I would jolt the gears as I changed them; the car would regularly stall; I would forget to check my blind spot or even look in the mirror. There just seemed to be too many little things to remember all at the same time, but I managed to pass my driver's test. Now that I have been driving regularly for the past twenty years or so, however, I can do all the things naturally and automatically that I had to concentrate so hard on doing at the start. I can even think about other things while I am driving.

The same is true of practising the character of God. Just as your fingers will flow with more ease over the keys of the piano with committed, continued practice, or you become more adept at driving the more you drive, so the practice of the character of God becomes your very nature the more you commit to it. Your inner self becomes the true self it was always meant to be; your heart becomes intertwined with God's, and your will becomes one with the Divine will. This means that in every part of your life, whether you are sitting in the sanctuary of a church or in some sacred holy site—or whether you are doing the dishes, vacuuming the house, sitting at your computer—or whether you are with your friends at a coffee house or having dinner with your family: you start, flow, and end every part of your life while naturally living out the character of God.

A word of warning, though: never condemn yourself when you fail to practise the Divine character. Remember this is a journey. We are *becoming* more like God, but we have not become like God yet. As Brother Lawrence said, "We need not be discouraged about our failures, but instead rely with total confidence on God's infinite abilities."

Allow the Divine character to develop in you and to develop you. Allow Christ to change and transform you.

MEDITATING ON GOD'S NAMES

Meditation on God's character doesn't mean we simply rehearse in our minds what we already think about God. Instead, we might use Lectio Divina to allow God's Name to take on new and ever deeper meaning within us. Here are some Divine names from the Hebrew Bible to get you started:

I Am
El Shaddai (the God Who Nourishes, Supplies, and Satisfies)
El Elyon (the Most High God)
Adonai (Lord, Master)
Yahweh (Lord, Jehovah)
Jehovah-Raah (the Lord My Shepherd)
Jehovah Rapha (the Lord That Heals)
Jehovah Tsidkenu (the Lord Our Righteousness)
Jehovah Mekoddishkem (the Lord Who Sanctifies You)
El Olam (the Everlasting God)
Jehovah Jireh (The Lord Will Provide)
Jehovah Shalom (The Lord Is Peace)

What does each of these names tell you about the Divine character? As you ponder each name, what does it reveal to you about God?

You might also want to come to Lectio Divina intentionally seeking to understand more about God's character. So, if for example, you are reading Psalm 48:14—*God is our God forever and ever; God will guide us until the end of life*—what can you learn about the Divine character? Or if you read 2 Corinthians 1:3—*God, the father of compassion, the God of every comfort and encouragement*—what can you deduce about God? Allow these insights to settle into you, deeper and deeper. See what they give rise to in your own heart. What do they ask of you?

10

Knowing God Through Creation: Meditating on Nature

I meditate on all your works
and consider what your hands have done.
—Psalm 143:5

Human beings have always found connections between the natural world and the spiritual world. As followers of Christ, meditating on creation has always been part of our spiritual heritage. When Jesus wanted to spend time alone with God, he sought out secluded places in the wilderness, where we're told he was alone except for the wild animals (Matthew 4). The ancient Celtic church, which thrived in the middle of the first millennium of Christianity, found deep spiritual meaning in the creation around them. One of the most ancient Celtic catechisms, attributed to Ninian who evangelized Scotland, asks, "What is the fruit of study?" The answer is:

"To perceive the eternal Word of God reflected in every plant and insect, every bird and animal, every man and woman." Columbanus, another great Celtic saint, said that if you truly want to get to know the Creator, then you must first get to know creation. The Celtic Christians were great missionaries, and they carried their faith around the world. Columbanus founded a monastery at Bobbio in northern Italy—and centuries later, Francis of Assisi, one of the best-known Christ-followers to connect nature and creatures to God, trained as a monk at Bobbio.

Although some modern Christians are leery of using creation as a vehicle for drawing close to God, meditating on nature is not at all the same thing as worshipping nature. Just as music, incense, and mantras can help us focus our minds, nature can also act as a tool that allows us to draw our thoughts into the presence of God. This is a biblical practice.

Jesus taught us to meditate on creation. In Luke 12:24, he told his disciples to "consider the ravens"; on another occasion, he said, "Consider the lilies of the field." The Greek word used in the Gospels for "consider" is *katanoeo*, which, according to Zondervan's *NIV Exhaustive Concordance*, is a word that "has a strong implication that the attention paid is intense, and the contemplation is broad and thorough, resulting in complete understanding." This is no fleeting glance upward at some black-feathered friends or a brief look at some pretty flowers. This is deep meditation on creation.

In Romans 1:20, the Apostle Paul gives his own teaching on creation meditation. He tells us that "by taking a long and thoughtful look at what God has created, people have always been able to see what their eyes as such can't see: eternal power, for instance, and the mystery of his divine being." (MSG). In the Hebrew scriptures (the Old Testament), David likens a thunderstorm to God's voice (Psalm 29:3–5 ESV):

> *The voice of the Lord is over the waters;*
> *the God of glory thunders,*
> *the Lord, over many waters.*
> *The voice of the Lord is powerful;*
> *the voice of the Lord is full of majesty.*
> *The voice of the Lord breaks the cedars;*
> *the Lord breaks the cedars of Lebanon.*

We can use nature as a trigger that turns our thoughts to God. Even if you live in a city, creation is everywhere, from sparrows on the pavement to blossoms on sale by flower sellers. The sky is a constantly changing panorama. Even the weather—rain and wind, sunshine and snow—can become vehicles of meditation. If nothing else, put on a nature DVD, with the sound turned down, and meditate on God's vast and lovely creation. Meditate on the world's beauty.

> *Beautiful it is that God shall save me.*
> *Beautiful too the bright fish in the lake,*

Beautiful too the sun in the sky,
The beauty of an eagle on the shore
when the tide is full. . . .
Beautiful the covenant of the Creator with Earth,
The beauty in the wilderness of doe and fawn,
The beauty of wild leeks and the berries of harvest,
The beauty of the heather when it turns purple,
Beautiful the pastureland. . . .
The beauty of water shimmering,
The beauty of the world where the Trinity speaks,
But the loveliest of all is the Christ
Who lives in all beauty.
—ancient Celtic poem

A MEDITATION WALK

As you first step onto the grass or into a forest, pause for a moment. Use the next step as a "crossing place" from your ordinary life into the presence, stillness, and tranquillity of God and creation.

Now, as you walk into the natural world, let your eyes scan your surroundings and take it in. What life can you see? What do you hear? What scents do you breathe? As you wander, with no definite destination in mind, allow the sounds of the outside world to fade away from your awareness. At the same time, as you take note of this, all the everyday concerns fade from your heart as you focus on God. Breathe deeply, quietly, and slowly as you walk. Do not speak out loud. Slow your physical pace. Remember: you have no goal to reach. You are not on a hike. You are not trying to burn calories or reach a goal. There is no rush. You are free to walk wherever you want (preferably away from roads).

Continue walking for at least an hour, stopping frequently to simply allow your senses to take in your surroundings. All the while, focus on:

God's creation: If you see something move—a bird, butterfly, squirrel, anything—stop and watch it. Watch it move; watch it when it is still. Look at the contrast of colours in the natural world: How many different shades of green do you see? How many subtle variations of gray and brown? Look at the sky. Pick something up—a stone, a leaf, a stick—and hold it in your hand, using it as a focal point for your meditation. Notice the intricacy and beauty of the natural world, and realise that you are a part of this intricate loveliness.

God's words: What does God say to you as you walk? Do you sense that you are beginning to see things through "new eyes"? Or are you simply enjoying Divine companionship? Reach beyond your physical senses; try to see and hear with the eyes and ears of your spirit. What does God say to you? Sit somewhere and just listen and watch.

Thank God: As you step out of the forest, park, or beach, pause again. Look back to where you have just walked. Think of all you have seen and heard, and open your heart to gratitude. What has God said to you in the quiet of your heart? What thoughts do you carry with you now?

The next step you take will bring you back into your ordinary world, but what messages do you bring with you? What thoughts will you continue to mull over, letting them sink deeper and deeper into your heart and mind? Take with you the peace you found during this time. Remember it, and come back in your memory to this place, the place in your heart, where this calm dwells.

The presence of God goes with you as you leave this quiet place. Do not leave it behind!

MEDITATIONS ON BIRDS

Scripture References

In the two parallel stories from Luke's Gospel and Matthew's Gospel, Jesus tells us to "consider the birds of the air" (Matthew 6:26, Luke 12:24). In Matthew 10:29–31, Jesus says, "Are not two sparrows sold for a penny? Yet not one of the falls to them ground apart from (or outside of) the will of your Father . . . so don't be afraid, you are worth more than many sparrows" (NIV).

The prophet Isaiah (40:28–31) tells us that those who are tired and weary can be renewed and soar on wings like eagles. Eagles and other raptors have a distinctive way of flying: they spread their wide wings and rest on the thermal currents. With very little effort, they hover far above the earth, upheld by the invisible wind.

And then, in the Hebrew scripture, we read the story of Elijah (1 Kings 17:1–6) in which God orders the ravens to feed him bread and meat twice a day.

Contemplate

Find a bird to watch. It could be pigeon or sparrow on a city street. It might be a robin in a hedge or a crow high up in a tree. You might watch it while sitting on a park bench, or you might see it from a window of your home. Wherever you are, focus your thoughts on this feathered creature. Let the rest of the world slip away from your awareness.

Now think about the Bible verses listed on the previous page. Dwell on the fact that all of creation is held in the Divine hand. Notice the energy and life within the bird you're watching, the sense of freedom and joyfulness. Consider the amazing ability of flight. Allow these thoughts to sink deep into your consciousness. Ask God to increase your confidence in Divine care. Pray for renewed strength. Ask that you might know how much God loves and cherishes you. Allow yourself to relax on the currents of the Spirit's breath.

Be like the bird who,
Pausing in her flight
Awhile on boughs too slight,
Feels them give way beneath her,
And yet sings,
Knowing that she hath wings.
—Victor Hugo

MEDITATION ON A ROCK

For this meditation, go and sit on a rock somewhere. If you can't do that, hold a stone in your hand.

Now focus your thoughts on the stone. Examine it with the tactile senses at the ends of your fingertips. Is the rock rough or smooth? Perhaps some parts are rough and others smooth. Does it have a subtle grain to it? Is it warm or cold? What are its colours? What is its shape? Contours?

Now think of this rock's history. What has been the physical journey through countless centuries that brought it here to this moment where you have encountered it? Is it igneous (formed by magma, molten lava solidifying above or below the Earth's surface)? Is it sedimentary (formed by particles of sand, mud, clay, or even animal or plant remains laid down in layers)? Is it metamorphic (rock that has been changed into another type by extreme heat or pressure)? Has it been shaped by wind and water? What forces have acted on it to make it take the shape it is now?

> *Consider the rock from which you were cut*
> *and the quarry from which you were hewn.*
> —Isaiah 51:1 (NLT)

In this passage, the prophet Isaiah was comparing the Jewish people's history to that of rock cut from a quarry. He was asking them to think about how they were formed and what in their past made them the people they were.

Meditating on Your Past

As you hold or touch the stone, begin to ponder your own history in reference to the verses below:

- God's loving creation of your uniqueness (Psalm 139:13–16)
- The path on which God has led you so far (Jeremiah 29:11)
- Divine patience as God works in your life (Philippians 1:6)
- Your spiritual ancestry: the things that are foundational to who you are (1 Peter 2:9–10)
- The experiences that have changed and re-formed you: the heat and pressure of life; the erosive forces that have damaged you or worn you down; the events and relationships that have changed your consistency, rounded or smoothed you (Romans 5:3–4)

Look for positive influences in your life for which you can give thanks. Look for jagged and distorted places that need God's healing or smoothing. Look for battered, worn, and weary places where you need the gentle renewing life of God. Look for the places where you know you are still a "work in progress" and ask God for the grace of continued transformation.

Listen to the voice of your own heart. Is God seeking to tell you something about your past? Is there something you need to learn about who you are and how you have become the person you are today?

If you know you have a particularly hard and painful history, do not attempt to go too deeply into your memories without help from someone you trust.

Meditating on the Future

In the midst of our changeable world, stone endures. The stone on which you are sitting or which you are holding in your hand will continue to exist in some form as long as the Earth does.

If God is your Rock and stronghold, what does that mean for your future? If the Divine is your ultimate strength and foundation, how does your perspective change when you consider your anxieties for the days ahead?

Praise God for the enduring strength of Divine mercy and providence. Remember this each time you see or hold this stone.

(Adapted from a meditation by Rev. Graham Booth, Guardian and Spiritual Director with the Community of Aidan and Hilda)

11

Showing the Mystic Path to a New Generation: Meditation with Children

Children are born contemplatives
and so contemplation is
not only the goal of the Christian life
but in a sense its starting point too.
—*Father Laurence Freeman*

I have two young children, so I understand that putting the words "meditation" and "children" in the same sentence might seem like craziness. But not only are there great benefits to be found in teaching children meditation, but I believe that meditation is something that is deeply rooted in practising an authentic Christ-centred faith—so if we want to teach our children to be authentic followers of Christ, if we want to teach them how to have a fulfilled relationship with God, then we need to teach them Christ-centred meditation.

This doesn't mean that I'm going to suggest that you insist your children sit and be quiet for long periods of time (although some children may be able to do that, or they can learn to do that). Many children seem to be physically incapable of sitting still for very long, and we don't want them to dismiss meditation as something that's boring and uncomfortable. Instead, we need to allow children to see that meditation is something that's enjoyable.

But why teach children to meditate when they're young? Why not assume that it's an activity they can learn more appropriately when they are older, when they have greater capacity to sit still and concentrate?

In Lorraine Murray's book *Calm Kids*, she offers three ways that meditation can benefit children. First, meditation can improve children's sleep.

> Meditation and mindfulness help to retrain the mind and body . . . which encourages longer and improved sleep . . . simple relaxation techniques before going to bed can become part of their established bedtime routines helping them to move into their deeper sleep state.

Second, meditation can help children manage their thoughts and feelings.

> Learning meditation helps children cope with challenges—encouraging their minds to develop

positive filters of their experiences and use this positive view to perceive the world. Meditation helps children stay grounded, let go of negative thoughts, process negative feelings and not become overwhelmed by normal aspects of life, like sitting exams or studying. . . . Gently encouraging the mind to become stronger and more focused is important for studying. Through meditation you will also help children to tap into their own creativity and imagination, which in turn will help them to discover solutions to problems and challenges they face in life.

And third, Murray states that meditation can give children a holistic sense of peace.

Thoughts can affect our physiological well-being, so if our children are worried about something it can affect their bodies too—tummy upset being a classic example. To change the way we think . . . we first have to become aware of the problem: we become aware, then we choose different thoughts. Only through awareness can we choose to change. . . . Perhaps you are thinking that you'd prefer your children not to notice how busy or negative their minds are and simply to shut out all these thoughts and have some peace and quiet! Suppressing worries can work in the short term, but meditation gives children a long-term support as they learn to change through awareness, using mindful activities for a sense of inner peace.

As parents, we want to give our children all the tools we can to be whole and healthy individuals, physically, emotionally, and spiritually. One of the most important things parents can do to encourage their children to meditate is to allow them to see their parents practising meditation; children naturally copy whatever they see their parents doing. I also actively encourage my children to engage in meditation to gain inner peace, and to practise mindfulness activities so that they can become more aware of the world around them. Even my five-year-old son can sit and listen for a moment or two. At bedtime, we do calming and stilling exercises—and in the morning, his visionary dreams can sometimes be quite enlightening!

A simple mindfulness exercise I play with my children is a game we call What Can You See? It's a bit like I Spy, but moves a little more quickly, and it gets my children very aware of the world around them. I start it off by looking around and saying something like, "I can see a man on a bike. What can you see?" We all look at the man on a bike and then one of my children will say something like, "I can see some purple flowers." And so on. The only rule is that we can't repeat anything that has already been "seen," so as the game continues, we have to become more and more aware of what is around us and ensure that our memory is engaged. We play this game as we walk along a path or travel in the car. It helps my children become more aware of the world around them, to really *look* and be aware of their surrounding, and to become more focused on the present moment.

Other activities can be equally effective. Some time ago I bought my daughter the *Personal Logbook for Children and Mentors* from the Transforming Church series by Ray Simpson. This is an activity book for children that contains ideas to stimulate young minds and encourages them to consider ways they can create a better world and become more holistically balanced people. It also gives children practical ideas and techniques for contemplative prayer. My ten-year-old daughter has a bean-bag chair in the corner of her room where she keeps this book, along with a graphic Bible; she goes there, on her own initiative, to absorb the Divine presence in simple stillness and mental activity. My wife and I would never tell her, "Now it's your meditation time. Go to your corner and meditate." This is completely self-initiated with no pressure attached.

Children are experiential. They learn best by doing, rather than from listening. Modern education has learned that child-initiated and interactive activities are the most effective lessons. We need to apply this same understanding of children's minds to their spiritual education. Children learn about Jesus and God most powerfully when they experience the Divine in their own hearts—rather than sitting and listening to Sunday school lessons and church sermons. Christ-centred meditation provides children with opportunities to journey to a place of inner silence and stillness where they will experience the Divine presence within their souls, as well as in the everyday circumstances of their lives.

Try to meditate regularly with your children, each morning and evening, when the family wakes up and before you go to bed. Routine is important for children, and also for the practice of meditation.

The World Community for Christian Meditation goes into schools and teaches children Christ-centred meditation. Here are some comments from the children they have taught:

I felt like I was in Jesus' house.

I felt God inside my heart.

When we meditate we are with God.

When I meditate I become calm and still.

Meditation allows children to discover the joys of dwelling in the Divine presence. It gives them the ability to manage their emotions better, to live less stressed lives, and to become acutely aware of the world around them, causing them to want to do what they can to make that world be a better place.

Teach them by example!

MEDITATION EXERCISE FOR CHILDREN

When you encourage children to meditate, meditate at the same time. Try this simple exercise:

Say to the children, "Sit down. Sit still and upright. Close your eyes lightly. Breathe calmly, deeply, and regularly. Silently, in your head, begin to picture somewhere peaceful. Maybe the beach . . . maybe the forest . . . maybe a clear blue pool."

After a couple of minutes, five minutes at most, ask the children with you to open their eyes again. If you practise this regularly, every day or so, children will learn to habitually go to this peaceful place in their minds. As they grow older, you can encourage them to return to this place when they start to feel anxious or worried at school or some other place, when they are about to take a test, or when they are about to do something that is a little scary for them. Developing the ability to retreat to an inner peaceful place can be of infinite benefit to them.

12

The Path to the Centre: Meditation's Goal

Contemplation is the highest expression
of man's intellectual and spiritual life.
It is that life itself, fully awake, fully active,
fully aware that it is alive.
It is spiritual wonder.
It is spontaneous awe
at the sacredness of life.
—*Thomas Merton*

In 1967, an eleven-year-old girl wrote to Thomas Merton, a Trappist monk and hermit, asking him for "any information whatsoever" to help her and her class study the concept of monasticism. The following is some of what Merton wrote back:

The monastic life goes back a long way. Monks are people who seek to devote all their time to knowing God better and loving him more. For that reason they leave the cities and go out into lonely places where it is quiet and they can think. As they go on they want to find lonelier and lonelier places so they can think even more. In the end people think these monks are really crazy going off by themselves and of course sometimes they are. On the other hand, when you are quiet and when you are free from a lot of cares . . . and when your heart is quiet, you suddenly realise that everything is beautiful and that just by being quiet you can almost sense that God is right there not only with you but even in you. Then you realise that it is worth the trouble of going away where you don't have to talk and mess around and make a darn fool of yourself in the middle of a lot of people who are running around in circles to no purpose. . . . I do not suppose for a moment that you wish to become a hermit . . . but anyway, I suggest that you sometimes be quiet and think how good a thing it is that you are loved by God who is infinite and who wants you to be supremely happy. (*A Life in Letters*, HarperOne, 2008)

Just as Thomas Merton said to this girl, I do not suppose that the majority of people reading this book want to become hermits. Neither do I. However, as Merton said, sometimes all of us need to "be quiet and think how good a thing it is that you are loved by God who is infinite and who wants you to be supremely happy." This is one of the reasons why I started to practise and teach Christ-centred meditation.

Dietrich Bonheoffer, a twentieth-century German priest who was killed for standing up against the Nazi regime, is credited with coining the phrase "New Monasticism," referring to individuals who find the idea of becoming a monk impossible, and yet for whom the ideals of monasticism resonate with their hearts. In New Monasticism, the concepts of "actual monasticism"—like a rule of life and a commitment to a rhythm of prayer and quiet contemplation—are set within the context of everyday life.

There are various ways to live out New Monasticism. Some people join lay orders, such as the Third Order Franciscans, or they join a dispersed community like the Community of Aidan and Hilda. Groups like this can provide members with a way of life, and other people to whom members can be accountable for living this out. Not everyone feels called to join one of these groups, however, and yet many people yearn for something more in their spiritual lives. They may feel dissatisfied with the spiritual direction they are receiving from their local churches. For these individuals, walking the mystic path of meditation can be another way to experience New Monasticism. In the words of Dietrich Bonheoffer:

The restoration of the church will surely come only from a new monasticism, which has nothing in common with the old, but a complete lack of compromise in a life lived in accordance with the Sermon on the Mount in the discipleship of Christ. I think it is time to gather people together to do this.

Jesus said that one of the reasons he came was to give us life in all its fullness (John 10:10). If we are to experience this abundant life that Jesus came to give us, then we must actively participate in all the aspects of a life lived in relationship with God. A fulfilled Christ-centred life means following all the teachings of Jesus, using his life as our example—including meditation and finding spaces for stillness and contemplative prayer.

Many of us have lives filled with commitments to our faith community. So many practical things need to be done. We feel pressured to be busy, busy, busy. We prove our commitment to our faith by how active we are. But we've allowed our society's values to infiltrate our churches. We're conditioned to believe that we can prove our worth by our achievements.

And our constant busyness can burn us out. It can drain us, leaving us nothing but resentment—resentment toward the people who don't do as much as we do, resentment toward those who ask us to do things, resentment toward the people who depend on us, resentment even toward God. Especially when things go wrong in our lives—for instance, we get sick because our bodies are worn out—we may feel as though God is being unfair. "I do so much for God—and this is the thanks I get!"

We need to find a healthy equilibrium in our lives. Just as we can't sit around meditating all day, we also need to stop *doing* during our every waking moment. We need to find a balance between being and doing. We need to become contemplative activists (a term coined by the Dominican Order).

If we are committed to following Christ, then we are called to a continued growth in our relationship with the Divine. In the Western church, however, we often face a great famine of practices that enable an authentic Divine deepening. Doctrine has often become the god of the church, and relationship has been replaced with "rightness." What is the *right* way to think about God, the *right* way to come into the Divine presence?

We don't often think of other relationships in these terms. Few of us, for example, would say, "I interact with my wife in these specific ways, and so everyone else should interact with their wives in exactly the same ways." We allow for privacy and spontaneity in our human relationships, and these elements are also necessary for true intimacy to grow. We need to feel the same respect for others' relationship with God, allowing it to grow and deepen in ways that are often hidden and private.

I'm not recommending, of course, that we condone or encourage destructive and unhealthy ways of interacting in our relationships with others and with

God; violence and neglect never build deeper relationships. And any relationship, whether human or Divine, requires an investment of time spent alone together. What happens during that time, however, is a private matter.

What all deepening relationships have in common is our commitment to surrender ourselves more and more to the other person. This is not to say that we lose our own identities—but that we are willing to become something more, together. This is what happens during Christ-centred meditation. As we walk the mystic path, we come to a place where we can interact directly, heart to heart, with God. Here we commune beyond the boundaries of doctrine, beyond what is right and what is wrong.

Here, as we lose ourselves in the Divine presence, we become our most authentic selves. We realise that the Divine presence of God is the same as the Divine image within us. This image resonates as one harmonious chord, a sacred and primal sound that fills the silence of Christ-centred meditation.

We begin our practice focusing on Christ; he is the centre point of our meditation. Then, as we continue, we realise that Christ is also the Way: he is the path that leads us into the Divine presence. And last, as we dwell there in the presence of God, the breath that breathes through us, resonating in our hearts, we realise that our breath is God's, and the sound of our hearts is the Divine heartbeat within us.

CHRIST-CENTRING EXERCISE

The following exercise is designed to be done repeatedly a few times a day over a period of days.

Close your eyes so that you are not distracted. Now imagine the Light of Christ descending slowly from the sky upon you, wherever you are in that moment. Recall Christ's words: "I am the Light of the world." Feel the Light as it surrounds you and encircles you. Breathe deeply as if you are breathing in the Light of Christ. Feel the Light as it enters your being.

Now sense within yourself all the things that have taken Christ's place at the centre of your life, all whirling around in chaos, causing you anxiety and discord within yourself. Picture the Light of Christ slowly and gently encircling and encapsulating them all and drawing them into one place. They are no longer whirling, they are no longer chaotic; instead, they are unified, enclosed in the Light of Christ. Allow this Light to move into your inmost centre. Feel the peace that comes from the knowledge that Christ has control of all things and that he is the centre of your life and being.

Stay in this place for a few moments. Then open your eyes, and, still centred of Christ's light, carry on with your day.

Here are some Lectio Divina verses to go with this exercise:

Psalm 37:7a

John 8:12

Philippians 4:6–7

1 Peter 5:7

May you know the Divine peace,
which transcends all understanding.

May you be aware of the Prince of Peace
walking with you and guiding you.

May you know the Spirit of God surrounding you,
filling you, and transforming you.

And may you allow God to show you new things
so you become truly enlightened.

God's first language is Silence.

Everything else is a translation.

—*Father Thomas Keating*

Appendix
Further Reading

Books

Many books have been written on the subject of meditation and Christ-centred meditation. The following is nowhere near an exhaustive list, but these are books I personally have found helpful. (They are listed alphabetically by the authors' surnames.)

Introduction to Contemplative Meditation by M.V. Dunlop
Labyrinth: Illuminating the Inner Path by Brian Draper
Celebration of Discipline by Richard Foster
Intimacy with God: An Introduction to Centering Prayer by Thomas Keating
The Practice of the Presence of God by Brother Lawrence
New Seeds of Contemplation by Thomas Merton
The Big Book of Christian Mysticism by Carl McColman

Finding Our Way Again: The Return of the Ancient Practice by Brian McLaren

Silent Waiting: The Biblical Roots of Contemplative Spirituality by Alexander Ryrie

At Sea with God by Margaret Silf

Landmarks: An Ignation Journey by Margaret Silf

Intimacy with the Almighty by Charles Swindoll

The Cloud of Unknowing by an Unknown Author

Ancient Faith, Future Mission: New Monasticism as Fresh Expression of Church by various authors

Online
Here are some websites I have also found helpful:

Anamchara, Carl McColman's website
anamchara.com

Calm Kids
teachchildrenmeditation.com

Centering Prayer (Thomas Keating's website)
centeringprayer.com

The Community of Aidan & Hilda
aidanandhilda.org

Mystic Christ
mysticchrist.co.uk

New Monasticism
newmonasticism.com

The World Community for Christian Meditation
wccm.org

The World Community for Christian Meditation (UK branch)
christianmeditation.org.uk

About the Author

David Cole has been learning and teaching Christ-centred meditation for many years now. He has worked in fulltime Christian ministry for the past twenty years. Currently, he is "Explorer Guide" with the Community of Aidan & Hilda (CA&H), a globally dispersed Celtic Christian community. In this role, he gives holistic life guidance to CA&H members as they apply the community's "Way of Life" to their everyday lives and spiritual journeys. The rest of his time is spent as a retreat leader, spiritual director, speaker, and teacher. He leads weekly classes, daylong seminars, and weekend and weeklong retreats on meditation.

David lives with his wife and children in the beautiful New Forest national park on the south coast of England.

ANAMCHARA BOOKS

BOOKS TO INSPIRE
YOUR SPIRITUAL JOURNEY

In Celtic Christianity, an *anamchara* is a soul friend, a companion and mentor (often across the miles and the years) on the spiritual journey. Soul friendship entails a commitment to both accept and challenge, to reach across all divisions in a search for the wisdom and truth at the heart of our lives.

At Anamchara Books, we are committed to creating a community of soul friends by publishing books that lead us into deeper relationships with God, the Earth, and each other. These books connect us with the great mystics of the past, as well as with more modern spiritual thinkers. They are designed to build bridges, shaping an inclusive spirituality where we all can grow.

You can order our books at **www.AnamcharaBooks.com**. Check out our site to read opinions and perspectives from our editorial staff on our Soul Friends blog. You can also submit your own blog posts by emailing **info@AnamcharaBooks.com** with "Blog Entry for Soul Friends" in the subject line. To find out more about Anamchara Books and connect with others on their own spiritual journeys, visit **www.AnamcharaBooks.com** today.

ANAMCHARA BOOKS
220 Front Street
Vestal, New York 13850
(607) 785-1578
www.AnamcharaBooks.com

Lightning Source UK Ltd.
Milton Keynes UK
UKOW041120240413

209670UK00001B/10/P